# The Star

# The Star

## & OTHER KOREAN SHORT STORIES

Translated from the Korean by

AGNITA TENNANT

KEGAN PAUL INTERNATIONAL
London and New York
UNESCO PUBLISHING
Paris

First published in 1996 by
Kegan Paul International
UK: P.O. Box 256, London WC1B 3SW, England
Tel: (0171) 580 5511 Fax: (0171) 436 0899
E-mail: books@keganpau.demon.so.uk
Internet: http://www/demon.co.uk/keganpaul/
USA: 562 West 113th Street, New York, NY 10025, USA
Tel: (212) 666 1000 Fax: (212) 316 3100

Distributed by

John Wiley & Sons Ltd
Southern Cross Trading Estate
1 Oldlands Way, Bognor Regis
West Sussex, PO22 9SW, England
Tel: (01243) 779 777 Fax: (01243) 820 250

Columbia University Press
562 West 113th Street
New York, NY 10025, USA
Tel: (212) 666 1000 Fax: (212) 316 3100

UNESCO COLLECTION OF REPRESENTATIVE WORKS
The publication of this work was assisted by a
contribution of the Government of the Republic
of Korea under UNESCO's Funds-in-Trust Programme



KEGAN PAUL INTERNATIONAL ISBN 0–7103–0533–8
UNESCO ISBN 92–3–103217–8

Set in 10/12 Bembo by Intype London Ltd

Printed and bound in Great Britain by
T. J. Press (Padstow) Ltd.



British Library Cataloguing in Publication data

Star and Other Korean Short Stories. –
(Unesco Collection of Representative Works)
I. Tennant, Agnita II. Series
895.730108 [FS]

ISBN 0–7103–0533–8

Library of Congress Cataloging-in-Publication Data

The star and other Korean short stories / translated from the Korean by
Agnita Tennant.
142pp. 21cm. (UNESCO Collection of Representative Works)
ISBN 0–7103–0533–8
1. Short stories, Korean—Translations into English. 2. Korean
fiction—20th century—Translations into English. I. Tennant,
Agnita, 1934–
PL984.E8S73 1966
895.7'30108—dc20

95–43446
CIP

# CONTENTS

# The Authors

Choi Hak was born in 1950 in Kyungsang-Pukdo. His writing career started in 1973 when he was awarded first prize for his novel in a competition organized by the daily paper, *Kyunghyang-shinmun*. Since then he had published several books including two historical novels *The North-West Wind* and *The Treason*, and also *The Sea that Wets the Rain, The Crying Fog* and *Winter Showers*. A collection of his short stories was published under the title *A Land for a Short Stay.* He was educated at Korea University and at present teaches at a technical college in Taejon.

'The Guest' in this collection was written in 1990.

Park Wan-suh was born in 1931 in Gaepyong-gun, Kyong-gi-do and was educated at Sukmyong Girls' High School and Seoul National University. She made her debut with a novel *The Naked Tree* in 1970. Her novels include *A Shaky Afternoon, It Was Warm That Winter* and *Arrogance and Illusion*. She has also written many short stories some of which were published under the titles *Shame is Being Taught, Stolen Poverty,* and *Spring Outside the Window.* She has received the Lee Sang Literary Award and the Literary Award of the Republic of Korea.

'She Knows, I Know and God Knows but . . .' was written in 1984.

Yi Chong-jun was born in 1933 in Chang-hung, Cholla-Namdo, educated at Kwang-ju So Middle School and Jeil High School, and studied German Literature at Seoul National University. He made his debut with a short story 'The Discharge' in 1965. He has written several novels including *Your Own Heaven* and *The Dancing*

*Priest*. Several collections of his short stories have been published under the titles *You Will Be Shown the Stars, Walls of Rumours, The Prophet, The Living Marsh* and *The Gate of Freedom*. He has received many prestigious literary awards including the Dong-in Literary Award, the Lee Sang Literary Award and the Literary Award of the Republic of Korea.

'Snowy Road' was written in 1977.

Im Chol-woo was born in 1954 on Wando Island off the coast of Cholla-Namdo. Since his debut with 'The Dog Thief' in 1981 he has written many stories, some of which were published under the titles *My Father's Land* and *The Beloved South*. He has also written a novel *The Red Hills, White Birds*. He was educated at Chon-nam and Sogang Universities and at present is a professor of English Literature at Chon-Nam.

'My Father's Land' was written in 1984.

Yang Guija was born in 1955 in Chonju, Cholla-Namdo and was educated at Chonju Girls' High School and Wonkwang University. Her writing career started with 'The Morning of a New Beginning' and 'The Door that is Already Closed', for which she was awarded the Yoo Ju-hyun Literary Award and the Lee Sang Literary Award. Her major works include the collections *Wonmi-dong People* and *The Deaf Bird*, and a novel *Hope*.

'The Poet of Wonmi-dong' was written in 1986.

Yoo Jai-yong was born in 1936 in Changdo, Kangwon-Do and was educated at Kyun-myong High School. He made his debut in 1969 with 'The Record of a Cohabitation'. His major novels include *The Holy Region, The Holy River, The Portrait of My Sister* and *Relationship*. His short stories were published in a collection entitled *The Man with a Tail*. He has been awarded the Lee Sang Literary Award, the Cho Yon-hyun Literary Award and the Literary Award of the Republic of Korea.

'The Star' was written in 1986.

Yoo Keumho was born in 1942 in Kohung, Cholla-Namdo. He made his debut in 1964 with a short story 'Colour the Sky', subsequently published in a collection with the same title. His novels include *The Winter Rain* and *Yonam, Park Jiwon*. He has also written books of literary criticism entitled *The Language, the Dream and the Disillusionment* and *A Study of Death as it Appears in the Korean Novel*. He was educated at Kong-ju Teachers' Training College and Korea University. He received a Ph.D from the latter and now teaches Modern Literature at Mokpo University.

'A Thin Line' was written in 1982.

Yoon Chongmo was born in 1946 in Wolsung, Kyongsang-Pukdo and educated at the Department of Creative Writing, Sorabol College of Arts. She made her debut in 1982 with *The Daughters of the Windy Corner*. Her works include several books of short stories: *The Night Road, Light* and *The Beloved*. She also has written several novels, including *The Islands, Then the Shouts Were Heard* and *The Fields*.

'Why the Silkworm Does Not Leave its Cocoon' was written in 1986.

# The Translator

Agnita Tennant, née Hong, was born in Korea and educated at Chong-ju Girls' High School and Yonsei University. She married an Englishman, Roger Tennant, and has lived in Leicestershire since 1964. She started translating Korean stories in the 1970s, and published a collection in 1972. Besides the present collection she has also translated the first volume of *Land*, a novel sequence by Park Kyong-ni, also published by Kegan Paul International.

She worked as a librarian for Leicestershire Libraries and Information Service until retiring in 1993. In 1990 she received a Ph.D. from Loughborough University for her study of Thomas Hardy's influence on Korean literature.

She has two children, Charlotte and Leo, who are both married.

# Translator's Preface

In recent years in the West the short story has somewhat lost its prestige. This collection, however, demonstrates that short stories can be complete, serious and rich in content and sophisticated in construction. They come from a literary tradition in which the short story is the most popular form of fiction. Korean short stories will, I believe, in due course, make a unique contribution to mainstream world literature.

Written by acclaimed contemporary writers, all winners of literary awards, these stories present deeply moving human dramas. What emerges from them is a picture of a somewhat sad people – sad because they have gone through sorrowful experiences of one kind or another. But they are people who transform their sufferings into blessings through their warm humanity, whether it be a soldier, a domestic servant or an office worker. And the source of this humanity, as we discover in these stories, lies in two things which are characteristic of the Korean people, namely powerful family bonds, intricately woven and enduring, and nostalgia for a past even though it might have been far from comfortable or glamorous, and was often extremely painful.

I have selected stories I believe are works of art and that will have a universal appeal. By chance, the eight stories reflect a common concern with the social realities of the 1980s. 'Snowy Road', 'The Star', 'A Thin Line' and 'The Guest' all have degrees of feeling for family ties and nostalgia. 'The Poet of Wonmi-dong' and 'She Knows, I Know and God Knows but . . .' present the age-old theme of the exploitation of the weak by the strong – in new clothes, as the exploiters are the new classes that have risen out of modern capitalism, industrialization and urbanization. A significant change in people's attitudes in regard to the Civil War is seen in 'My Father's Land' and 'Why the Silkworm Does Not Leave its Cocoon'. The War is reassessed from a nationalist stance. The North, with which the South had waged fierce battles, is no longer seen as 'the enemy', but rather as an ill-divided part of one nation. An awareness emerges that all the cruelty and loss of life was for no good purpose but rather an internecine family feud.

Each of these stories will, I believe, speak for itself, even for readers without any background knowledge of the country.

# THE STAR

## Yoo Jai-yong

OF all the children, Daisik was the only one who actually saw it happen. The other boys who had been waiting out on the main road for the bicycle people to come by had scattered and gone home for lunch. At about this time of day there were not many of them anyway, probably because they were stopping to eat, their bicycles propped up, at the market square in Baigam, four miles away. As I hadn't been able to do more than one run all morning, I was particularly anxious to get lunch over so that I could be back before the others, to wait for them.

'Don't strain yourself, dear,' said my mother as she came out of the kitchen with my food table. 'I am just grateful that all my family have survived through this summer. Besides, your father says we may be able to go home soon if things turn out right.' The subject of going home again was always welcome. I wouldn't have minded being woken up even in the middle of a sweet sleep if it was about that. Even so, I dumped my rice into the bowl of water and almost gulped it down as if it was a sweet bowl of *sikey*, and rose to my feet, for 'going home' and helping to push the bicycles had nothing to do with each other.

I did up my belt and was about to step down out of the house when the sound of a shot shook the whole earth. 'Shook' is an understatement. It sounded as if it was tearing it into shreds. Rifle fire was not an unfamiliar sound to us. All through the summer, since the start of the war, we had heard it often enough. But that shot sent a chill through my heart – perhaps because it sounded so close, particularly now, when we had begun to think that such things had gone far away.

I leapt down the step to run across the yard and out of the gate.

I stopped there and took a quick glance in the direction of the main road that passed the village. The shot had come from that direction. I noticed the *Taigukki*, the Southern flag, flying from the pole in front of the town hall. I was sure that it hadn't been there when I had been coming home for lunch shortly before. I guessed that the Southern army or its outrunners must have arrived. News had been spread around that along with the UN, forces they had landed at Inchon, had recaptured Seoul, and were moving north toward the thirty-eighth parallel, but here in Jwahangli there had not yet been any sign of them or the police.

The Northern police, occupying the local station deserted by the South, had reigned mercilessly, but now it was the interim between their running away and the return of the Southern forces. I had often seen the shabby backs of stragglers from the defeated Northern army, said to have disappeared northwards beyond the Doechangmal hill, but I had not yet sighted the other army triumphantly marching in. I told myself that they were probably the ones who, returning, had put up the flag and, overcome with emotion, had fired the shot.

I was about to hurry on again towards the hall when I saw Daisik come running round the corner of the mud wall of the house next door. He was all out of breath. His first words were, 'Someone's been killed!' His face was pallid with fright.

Restraining my urge to run I asked, 'Killed? Who has?'

'Bong-tai's dad. He was shot straight through the forehead and died at once.'

He was about to run into his own house but the next moment he snatched my hand and led me inside my grandmother's, where my family were staying. Here he told me what he had just seen.

He had come home for lunch but had not even bothered to sit down. Instead he had taken the steamed potatoes that his mother had prepared, some in his pocket and some in his hands, and gone straight back to the main road. He had thought he might find some odd bicycle people who, after eating early, would be passing by. As he chewed his potatoes he kept glancing up the road that stretched to the south. With a scattering of poplars standing along either side, it ran straight alongside the fields up to the approaches of Mirok village, at which point it curved round the corner of a hill and slid its tail out of sight. There was not one cyclist to be seen on this stretch of road, only a couple of people on foot. I should have eaten my lunch in comfort at home, he thought, as he turned his eyes towards the village. Being lunch-time, that lane was deserted too. Then, on this quiet lane, he saw Bong-tai's father and Minsik's father walking up, talking to each other as they went.

Instead of coming up to the main road they went up to the town hall which was only about twenty paces away from it, a distance you could reach with your nose if you fell flat. They went up to the flagpole and fastened a flag on the rope that dangled from it. It was the flag of the South. They pulled the rope to draw it up to the top. A few days before it had been the flag of the North that had hung there. The one who had fastened it on the rope and raised it had also been Bong-tai's father. Now, as if he was intending to wait until such time as the village people would notice that it was he and his friend who had put it up, he squatted beneath it.

They took out their tobacco pouches and rolled cigarettes. It was as they were bringing them to their lips that the strangers appeared. One of them was tall and looked elderly and the other was short and youthful. Though wearing civilian clothes, each of them had a rifle. Without seeming to notice the existence of Daisik, they walked briskly up to the hall.

'Who put up this flag?' asked the taller and older man as he stood before them.

'I did, sir.' Bong-tai's father, as if he was being complimented, gave a shy smile as he rose to his feet.

'Reactionary bastard!' No sooner had the tall man shouted this than a shot rang out as if to pierce one's eardrums. The body of Bong-tai's father fell backwards like a rotten tree trunk. Then the men with guns, as if frightened by what they had done, turned and began to run in the direction of Doechangmal hill, leaving behind the *Taigukki* still forcefully flapping in the wind.

The taller and older one who had fired the shot ran well as he was sturdily built, but the smaller and younger one, as he followed, seemed to struggle as if he were tender and weak. He kept falling behind and the other one kept urging him on. After a while they were hidden by the curve of the hill.

The forehead of Bong-tai's father was all messed up. When Minsik's father recovered his wits, he picked up the blood-covered body of his friend, no longer of this world, put it over his shoulder and took him to his house. Up to this point this was what Daisik had told me.

'Who was it who shot him?' Curious, I asked.

'Must be a member of the Northern police or a soldier I suppose. Because when he killed him he called him a reactionary bastard for putting up the *Taigukki.*'

His eyes still showed lingering traces of fear and at the same time satisfaction at his fortune in witnessing something that others had not, so that he could report it, or perhaps his look of satisfaction came from a sense of relief at his narrow escape from death. Foolishly, I was aware of envy stirring within me, and to hide it I said, 'Of all people, why should Bong-tai's father be shot? Doesn't it seem strange?'

I saw before my eyes the sight of Bong-tai's father on his knees touching the floor with his forehead again and again as he begged forgiveness from my grandfather on the morning when he had come to see him a few days ago. 'Sir, I am an ignorant man, as ignorant as if I was blind. I am old but foolish in mind, so I have sinned. Please forgive me, sir, with your generous heart, for you are as merciful as the Buddha. I will never do such things again.' He had repeated these phrases ten times or more and went away only after having heard my grandfather say, 'The times are more to be blamed than you. Anyway, if you repent of what you have done that is all that matters. You had better go home now.' I found out later that he had been round the whole village calling on every house to beg forgiveness in the same way.

During the few months in the summer when, following the invasion by the Northern army, the Communists reigned over the world, Bong-tai's father, wearing a red arm-band, had worked for them, literally as an errand boy.

'I have to tell you that there is a meeting tonight. You are asked to come to the primary school.' I could still hear his polite yet churlish voice as he thrust his head from behind the gate while we were all sitting round the table eating our supper. The reason he was passing the message on about the time when people sat round the supper table was said to be because he could go round on errands only after he had finished his own work at home. So he went round the village in the dusk, half running, on legs as thin as a heron's. Besides this, he had another task, which was to listen out for the sound of aeroplanes outside the school while after supper the villagers gathered inside to listen to the speeches given by young people with red arm-bands, or learn to sing the Northern songs. He stood there, and when he heard a plane he shouted 'Air raid!'. At his signal the lights went out in the class room, coming on again when he shouted 'All clear!'.

Sometimes this happened several times on one night, and the only assistance he ever gave the authorities under the Communist regime was in trivial tasks like this. In the eyes of the villagers what he was doing did not seem particularly odd or surprising, like the cases of some others, for he had eked out his living by doing the same kind of jobs even before the coming of the Northern army. He had a large family with very little land, three *majigi* paddy and three hundred *pyong* of dry land. To make up for the shortage of food, he cut people's hair for which he was paid with grain in the autumn, and was called out by families in the village when they needed extra hands. He helped out and earned some pocket money.

Then came the news that the Northern army, bragging that they would soon take Pusan, the South's temporary capital, had completely collapsed and were in retreat. With this news the Northern police, who had been all-powerful, disappeared overnight like water leaking out, and then Bong-tai's father, as if he alone had committed sins that deserved death, had gone from house to house to beg forgiveness. The villagers who had never thought of him as having sinned against or wronged anyone easily forgave him. Had he thought that even then it was not enough to atone? The idea of putting up the Southern flag on the flagstaff of the town hall could be seen as a further act of atonement.

Because of this affair I put aside all thought of catching the bicycle people for several hours. Someone has died, so who cares about them? At the same time my head was filled with the fear that an assassin, whether a member of the Northern army or the police, might appear and shoot again.

After Daisik had gone inside saying, 'I am not going to work any more today,' I sat on the verandah of the outer rooms looking in the direction of the main road. The flag was no longer there – someone had taken it down. Not only that, but the whole village was quiet. Even though Bong-tai's house was some distance away one might have expected to hear a sound of keening from there on the wind but there was none. Were they smothering their grief? Perhaps the whole family were dazed by what had happened so suddenly and so monstrously that they were hardly able to tell whether it was dream or reality. As for me, I kept feeling as if I was in a dream. It seemed weird that somebody had died and yet all around should be so quiet.

At last I caught a glimpse of a bicycle passing on the main road to the back of which was attached a child of about my own age. Even while I was thinking it was a strange sight to see a loaded bicycle being pushed from behind I suddenly came to my senses. That, despite the fact that a man who had been alive and well a short time before now lay dead, brutally and unjustly murdered, daily life still carried on as usual – this filled my heart with sorrow, but at the same time it had a calming effect. That's it. There is no need to feel guilty towards Bong-tai's family for pushing bicycles and getting paid for it. They are two different matters. I got to my feet and started towards the main road.

'Look, Myongsoo. Where do you think you are going?' As if she had been keeping an eye on me, my mother came so far as the outside of the gate to ask.

'I was just going to have a look round the village.' I made up in my confusion. 'Come back soon, won't you? It's better not to roam around on a day like this.'

'Yes, mother,' I said, without looking back. When I thought her eyes were no longer on me I turned towards the main road.

I don't remember exactly how long it was since people had started to move along it with loaded bicycles or how it all began that the village children came to be helping them by pushing their bicycles from behind as a way of earning money. Before the war there were never any cyclists to be seen. Even in the early days of the war there was still none. Probably it was only after the Northern armies had penetrated deep into the South that the cyclists began to be seen on the road that passed Jwahangli village.

One day, Daisik had said, 'Myongsoo, I am on my way to push the bicycles. Why don't you come too? If you push them right up to the top of Doechangmal hill they give you money.' Apparently he had started the day before. I had followed him to the road. Lined up along both sides of it were boys of about our own age, fifteen . . . or sixteen-year-olds from the village. Their eyes were fixed on the main road to the south. In the far distance black dots flickered. They grew bigger and bigger until they turned into approaching bicycles. They were heavily laden with stuff. The boys ran towards them.

'Mister, let me give you a push.'

'How much do you want?' the owner would ask as he got off

his bicycle. The upward incline started from the village. Even without the children blocking his way he would have had to dismount anyway.

'A hundred and fifty *won*, please.'

'Let's make it a hundred.'

'No, we won't. You know very well how steep it is.'

Doechangmal hill was made up of three long curves and they said it was a mile from the village to the top.

'All right. A hundred and fifty. Come on, push.'

When the bargaining was done, with the owner holding the handlebars in front and the child pushing from behind, the uphill climb began. Of the three or four children who rushed to each cycle, only one would be chosen, but the others did not despair. The cyclists came constantly. I was told that if you were keen and quick you would have the chance of pushing one as often as six times a day, or the slightly slower ones, about four times. At last my chance came. Partly because most of the children had already gone up there was now little competition.

'Mister, would you like me to push?' Feeling a little shy I spoke in the Yongin accent of my home town.

'How much?'

'Only a hundred and fifty *won*, sir.'

'Let's make it a hundred.'

'No, we can't. You know very well how steep it is.' I just copied the fashion of the others.

'All right, then. Come on, push.'

Stuck behind the bicycle, I began to push. The loads were grain. Two large sacks of rice or barley were stacked one on top of the other. It was not as easy as it looked. Besides, I was tense and over-energetic at the thought that it was my first job. By the time I had pushed it up to the top and turned to go down again my legs felt wobbly. However, there was in my pocket a smart one hundred and fifty *won*, the first money that I had ever earned in all my life. My happiness far outweighed my tiredness.

After that I had been out every day to stand about waiting for them. I was on the slow side so four times a day was the most I could manage, but I had developed some shrewdness so that if I was too tired on the way to the top I earned a break by claiming a call of nature and pretending to urinate. I also found out that what they were carrying was grain they had managed to get hold of in the countryside and were taking up to Seoul to sell. To the south the road went through Baigam and Juksan to Jinchon and Eumsong in Chungchong province, and to the north it passed over the Doechangmal hill and at the village of Yongji joined up with the main road that linked Suwon and Yoju. The cyclists, I learned, would go from Yongji in the direction of Suwon and somewhere between Yongji and Sin-gal turn into Maljukkori and Sobingo, and from there on to the road to Seoul. It was a time when there was no sign of ordinary cars, only army vehicles on the roads. I often wondered about the price of rice in the Seoul markets that had been carried there on bicycles, but I had never asked the question.

The blood of Bong-tai's father that had stained the ground in front of the flag-pole at the town hall was no longer visible. Some one had covered it over with soil. Now and again children cast quick glances in that direction, but more often their eyes were fixed for a longer time on the road. The murderer had gone off over the hill a few hours ago and now that the blood was covered over and no longer visible did the boys who had not actually witnessed the incident themselves think that it was all over? During the summer they had heard too many stories of people being shot and seen as many themselves. As if each one was saying to himself that it had not been all that serious, not serious enough to give up the job of pushing bicycles, they were taking them on and walking one by one up the slope.

The sun was low on the western mountain. Because of that incident, I thought, I won't be able to do it more than once. To push a bike up the hill and then walk down again would take more than an hour. Even if I set off right now the sun would be sinking by the time I got back. I looked down the road to the south. A bicycle was speeding along. I leapt towards it, though getting there first did not always mean that your job was guaranteed, for the cyclist, on his side, could choose the one he liked best.

'Can I give you a push?'

'If you are sure you can make a good job of it,' said the cyclist as he brought his machine to a halt.

'Of course I can.' I started pushing. It was loaded with no fewer than three sacks of rice. Even though it was only a matter of making the wheels go round, pushing it up the steep slope was hard work. Why couldn't I have got one with two sacks instead of three? I grumbled to myself as I pushed away. Perhaps because

I was pushing so hard, I started to feel a mild stomach-ache and my tummy muscles were stiffening by the time we were half-way up. Perhaps that was because in my eagerness to get lunch over quickly I had swallowed the cold rice without sufficiently chewing it. By the time I was on my way down again the pain was quite acute. I decided that I could not just leave it till I got home. I went off the road on to the side of the hill where there was a scrub of mixed trees such as pine and oak.

After picking up a handful of pine leaves to wipe my bottom I was looking for the right place to squat. I saw a flat secluded spot by a large boulder. I was going to hide myself behind it while I got on with it.

'Don't move!' The barrel of a rifle was aimed at my heart. It was a boy like myself, about fifteen, or at most a year or two more, but his eyes were as murderous as the gun barrel. Flabbergasted I held my hands high.

'Are you by yourself?'

'Yes, sir.'

'What did you come here for?'

'On the way down I needed a shit. I was looking for the right place.'

'Don't lie, you bastard! You're looking for someone, aren't you? You're not alone, are you? Tell the truth.' He thrust his gun even closer to my chest. I felt as if there would be a bang at any moment and the bullet would tear it apart.

'I'm all by myself. I really did come just to shit.' My voice shook with tears.

'If you don't tell the truth I'll kill you. Where have you been?' The end of the gun jabbed at my heart. I told him with much stammering how I had been pushing the bicycle, as I swallowed hard the fear that was choking me.

'Idiot, sit down and shit then!' His gun was still pointing at me. I realized that the urge to relieve myself had gone. My stomach-ache had disappeared as well. But lest I be suspected of lying I pulled down my trousers and squatted down. What if it doesn't come? I was worried, but fortunately it did. I wiped my bottom with the pine leaves I had in my hand. As I stood up thoughts of what might happen to me flashed across my mind.

'Idiot, cover it up and walk on in front of me,' he ordered. As I was told, I scooped up some earth with my hand to cover it and then walked on deeper into the woods.

'Stop! Sit down,' he said from behind. Again it was beside a boulder. I sat down and heard him sitting also behind me. Between the trees I could see the golden fields in front of the village down below. At the foot of the hill the sun had already gone and darkness was falling fast. From the chimneys rose the smoke of supper cooking and following the wisps of the smoke, the darkness came higher and higher. The main road before the village was empty with not one cyclist or child in sight. Beside the main road I could see the town hall lying low and flat. I could vividly imagine the *Taigukki* that had been up on the flag-pole and hear the sound of the gun. No sound came from behind me. I kept my mouth shut. Suddenly it crossed my mind that it must be one of the two strangers who were said to have shot Bong-tai's father and had disappeared behind the hill. If so, I wondered, why had he let the taller and older one who had fired the shot go off and leave him here by himself? The sunset that had inflamed the western sky was now extinguishing itself. The village that had been pervaded by shadows was now immersed in darkness. I felt as if the sight of the village and the fields was about to disappear from my sight for good. Will I ever see my parents and my sisters and brothers again? Longing for them, sorrow and fear were gnawing at my heart.

Memories rose of the time when we were escaping from the North across the 38th parallel three years before. After waiting till deep in the night my family had set off, following the guide who walked before us. People from other places joined us to form a long line. It was a dark night with no moon. Lest I should lose sight of the dark back of the person in front of me I was absorbed in walking for some time when I realized that the long line of people had been cut somewhere behind me and I was separated from the rest of my family. We stopped and waited for them to catch us up, but they never did for they had gone off on another track. We could not wait endlessly, they said, so I had to follow them and go on. The yearning for my family, the sorrow and the fear as I walked amongst strangers suddenly came back to me. After dawn I had been able to rejoin them on the other side of the line.

When towards the end of last June the Northern army had occupied Seoul, I was separated from my family, who were staying with my maternal grandparents. During those few days before I could rejoin them, especially in the dark nights as I tossed about unable to sleep, longing, sorrow and fear had filled my heart till I felt it would burst.

The darkness had now reached my feet. All I could see below was a blackness like the sea. Even the peaks of the mountains that stood out like islands were melting and flowing into the darkness. From behind me came now and again only the sound of the gun tapping lightly against the rock, but not a word. Unable to stifle the tears that suddenly surged up, I let out a sob. It brought me the courage to speak. 'Please let me go. My mother is waiting for me, can't you see it?' It was a voice choked with tears. There was no response for a long time until I heard him mutter to himself. 'Mother . . .'.

It went all quiet again. There was only the light knocking of the gun on the rock now and again. By now darkness filled the sky and everything that had been visible was submerged. From a far distance came the call of an owl, strange to the ear, as if from another world. Cold air swept down the back of my neck and round my chest and back. Suddenly there was a sound from behind, a sound as light as that of two feathers brushing against each other. I pricked up my ears. There it was again. It was the sound of a deep sigh being released. It was hardly audible, yet not a light sound. Was it a sigh released at the thought of his home and his mother?

'What is on the other side of this hill?' he asked abruptly.

'At Yangji the path meets the road between Suwon and Yoju.'

'Let's move,' came from behind.

'Pardon?' I seemed to hear my heart sinking with a crash.

'Walk in front until we come to the top of the hill.' As I led the way out of the woods I felt my heart and legs juddering wildly. I remembered people saying that if you show the way to escaping soldiers you will be killed by them for if they let you go you'd tell their pursuers which way they had gone. I wanted to bolt into the darkness. Even if I was sure I would be killed at least I ought to try and escape. If I was lucky I might even survive. But I didn't dare to. He was following close behind me with the gun. We reached the top of the hill.

'That will do. You can go back now.'

'You mean go home?' I asked unsure.

'Where else have you got to go to? Off you go, quickly!' Horror enwrapped my whole body. I thought he will stab me in the back with a knife he has kept hidden the moment I turn my face. Or shoot me. Reluctantly, I turned and started to walk away. My legs were wobbly. Either the knife will come or the report of a gun. But nothing happened before I had turned the first bend. By the time I reached the gate of the house my whole body was drenched in sweat.

# MY FATHER'S LAND

## Im Chol-woo

THE truck was slowly crawling along the yellow road that stretched between the fields a little way from us, like a beetle lumbering away. Each time the wheels bounced on the uneven surface you could hear the clanking of metal, and whitish dust rose behind. The figure crouching alone in the uncovered rear of it looked pathetically small and shrunken. The aluminium food containers, also loaded in the back, now and again cast a cold metallic glint. In the still landscape of the hills and fields of early evening, the blades of grass losing their sparkle, and on the hills the colours little by little turning ashy, it was the only thing that moved as it persistently wriggled onwards. 'Poor chap – having to face a funeral only fifteen days after his transfer,' mumbled Private Oh, as he undid his trousers to pee. Without speaking, I crushed a dry blade of grass between my teeth. We had just got off the truck. Soon after leaving the camp we had reached the entrance to this small path that led up to the village, where our senior officer had stopped the vehicle to drop us off.

By now the truck was beyond the fields and about to turn the corner of a hill. I did not even know the name of the newly transferred man. All I remembered was my first sight of him on the day he had arrived, shortly before the start of field training. Hugging a duffle bag, he had stepped awkwardly into the untidy barracks where I was busily engaged in packing and preparing. In the back of the supply lorry that appeared at the camp every other day he was now on his way to the Headquarters. As soon as he got there he would be granted special leave and then he would be dashing for home, probably too late. On his arrival he would find the burial was over and the white awning that had been put up in the yard taken down. Now, when at last the lorry and its trail of dust had disappeared, the empty landscape awkwardly settled back into place.

'Poor boy. I feel sorry for him,' Private Oh said as he did up his trousers. 'Tall and thin as he is, he was ready to burst into tears. Apparently his mother was a widow.'

We started to walk. Across the low hill on the right-hand side of the military road there was a path just about wide enough for a car to pass through. At the entrance stood a waist-high concrete sign on which a rough hand had written in green against the background of white paint '*Saemaul* Anti-Communist Village'. We turned into the path and walked up the shallow incline. The stream that ran beside it was almost dried up. We followed the forlorn approach with scrubby oak and alder here and there and had just reached the top of the rise. Suddenly, before our eyes, there shot into the air a host of dark lumps, and as if by a prearranged signal we jumped back a pace.

It was a flock of crows. On either side of the road lay quite extensive fields. Mooli and cabbages that had missed the harvest lay rotting in the furrows after being struck by the frost. Wherever they had come from, countless crows had gathered to turn over the furrows, flapping their sinister black wings. Frightened by the sound of our approach, they had fluttered into the air. The rascals didn't go far – just to the end of the plantation where they turned and landed back on the soil again one by one, their wings flapping like pieces of black cloth. Some of them cast suspicious glances in our direction now and again but nevertheless they carried on scavenging with their backs turned.

Private Oh threw stones at them. Scattered here and there like lumps of charcoal their sluggishly moving bodies rose all at once into the air with a screech. 'Caw! Caw!' The sound shook the infinitely desolate early winter fields. He now picked up smaller pebbles to aim at them as they flew away but the missiles did not even reach the end of the field before they dropped to the ground.

'Even the damned crows are trying to upset me today.' He spat loudly as he picked up the rifle he had laid down. There were ominous black spots in a corner of the sky as the countless birds circled a couple of times over our heads before they finally took off for the edge of the hill on the other side of the field. Each flap of their wide wings roused in us an eerie repulsion as if something might rain down on us, and our necks flinched.

'If only I had some bullets,' he said, 'I would just . . .'.

'Don't let it bother you. It's a long time since I last saw any. I am rather pleased to see them, I must say.'

'Pleased? To see those bastards who peck out the eyes of dead men and eat them? They say magpies are a good omen, but I detest even them. A bird should be small and pretty. What kind of birds do you call them with black . . .'. I smiled to myself as I looked at his helpless look of anger. I could understand how badly he had been upset. His expression earlier in the day floated back to me. He was digging away when suddenly he gave a dreadful scream, threw away his shovel, and ran from the spot.

'It's all right, man. Haven't you ever seen anyone's bones before?' His colleagues had teased him and he had broken into a faint, embarrassed smile, feigning calm on the surface, but obviously unable to wipe out the unpleasantness. Even now he spat again and again as he walked in front of me with his head slightly bent.

'To begin with,' he said as he kicked away a dry twig, 'I had a nasty dream last night, damn it.'

'What was it about?'

'I saw a bier, didn't I? The weird thing was that it wasn't even a hearse or an ambulance but an old-fashioned bier all coloured in red and blue and green, and as I walked behind it I was crying loudly. Then I woke up. In fact, I've never seen a bier in my life except in films. Isn't it weird?' He turned round as he asked me, his face showing that he was really puzzled and troubled.

'Your dream turned out to be right then. It's just that you dreamt it on behalf of that other chap.' While I answered like this I was perfectly well aware of what he was thinking about. He obviously had something else in mind as he sulkily shut his mouth.

With each step we took our rifles struck the water flasks on our waists and gave out a clanking sound. Turning round I saw the flock of crows come fluttering down to land in the fields we had just passed. They probably had a secret store of food there. The sight of all .these large birds, evil-looking and sly, moving about in a flock of their own kind in the bare and empty fields of early winter, sluggishily strutting between dry furrows that seemed to hold nothing made me melancholy for no obvious reason.

'Look at them! You see, birds know the changes of the seasons before we do,' said my mother. She had been putting out small pieces of sweet potato, one by one, on top of the stone wall in the front yard to dry them in the sun. Squatting on the mud floor of the room watching a dragonfly, I lifted my head indifferently. She was leaning against the fence, looking up at the sky with her head tilted back. Her eyes were fixed on what at first glance looked like innumerable tiny specks in the sky. It was a flock of birds. Looking more carefully, they had long necks. They could be the wild geese or cranes that we had learned about in our nature lessons, I thought. With no signs of haste they flew steadily across the sky.

Every year at about the time when the woods in the hills that faced our village began to be tinged with yellow and the autumn sun was slowly losing its heat, I often saw coming over the ridge of the mountains behind the village formations of migrating birds. They flew over very high with their necks stretched out. There were many of them, and they flew on and on incessantly. I already knew that these birds came from behind the hills and flew on over our village towards the sea that lay beyond.

'Listen to me my child. They are seasonal birds migrating from the north. As the weather gets colder they go south where it is mild and then come back to their old home when spring returns.' My mother, like someone whose soul has gone out of her, forgetting her work and with her neck still stretched backwards, stared into the sky as she spoke. I even knew such details as that these birds lived by the sea feeding on things like small fish, water snails and shell-fish, but I did not rudely interrupt her for I had now heard several times before the exact same words. By now I had come to accept that they were for her a kind of incantation.

I returned to my dragonfly. Holding its wings pinned between my knees, I was trying to tie a length of thread to one of its legs. Because it kept wriggling as its bulging eyes rolled round, I was finding it very difficult. With the help of this one I meant to lure more dragonflies.

My mother went on standing like this for a long time, still staring into the sky. But the birds never bothered to cast so much as a glance at us and kept on passing over our heads towards the sea. It made my anger brim over for no obvious reason, so I sent some potatoes flying after them. My mother stood as if fixed for a long, long time until they had all passed over the plantations in the village and disappeared, flickering behind the ridge of the hill. Then she would mumble to herself as if suddenly remembering.

'That's right. It's a law of nature that even flying creatures like these know the right time to come home. Just look at them, coming all this way with such great effort and perseverance, coming from northern parts that are far far away.'

At times such as this she seemed to be entranced. Her talk was not necessarily for me. Sometimes it sounded more as if it was aimed at the birds as they flew in formation in one long line or in the shape of an L or an arrow head, and at other times it was as if she was having a conversation in a low voice with someone who she alone knew.

Suddenly the houses, closely set, came into view a short way ahead. It was a village of approximately thirty families. On the embankment of a small river made up of streams that had found their way down through the mountain valleys and now skirted the village stood lanky willows widely spaced, all bare. It had without exception the features you can see in villages everywhere these days – houses, old and shabby, with tiles or corrugated iron clumsily put over the old roof and painted thickly in primary colours. It made them look unfriendly, and almost evil. For a village among the valleys of such a mountainous province as Kangwon-do, the fields around were on fairly level ground. It was from these that the villagers eked out their living. At a first glance one could see that it was a lonely and isolated place, thoroughly infested with poverty.

As we passed a house that stood apart from the main group without even a fence, a dog rushed out from a shabby room with an earthen floor to bark at us. It was an emaciated, ugly-looking mongrel. At the entrance to the village was a tiny shop, probably the only one around. There was a metal sign with the word 'tobacco', and beside it, stuck on the wall, a red mailbox. It would be the best place to enquire.

There was an old and ill-fitting glass door which was closed, with no sign of life anywhere around, making you wonder whether the houses in the neighbourhood were all empty. Private Oh unslung his rifle and took off his helmet and after putting them on the dusty trestle table set out in front of the shop, sat sideways to smoke. I peered through the glass panes. There were thick layers of dust on the sills. No one was visible inside. Only by pushing the door did I find it was not locked. It could hardly be called a shop. There were a few packets of cheap biscuits in a cardboard box and also on display were bottles of *soju*, packets of noodles, soap, matches and some elastic bands – that was all. After I had called out several times, a latticed paper door, pasted over with several layers, opened half-way to reveal a human head sticking out of the gap. It was that of an old woman whose hair was half white.

'What do you want?' she said. Only when she recognized our army uniform did she move up sluggishly to the threshold, her hand still holding on to the door handle. Inside the dusky room I could not make out whether there was anyone else. I could see the end of a shabby quilt laid out on the floor.

'Excuse me, m'am. May I ask you something?'

'What about?'

As I took off my helmet I tried to put a smile on my face. I could see from her expression that she was still regarding us with suspicion. I asked where the head man of the village lived.

'The head of the village? I don't know what it's about but you wouldn't see him even if you went there . . .'. She then let go of the door handle. At the same time, with a squeak, it opened further. 'He called during the morning and I gather he has some business in the town. The last bus doesn't get here before dark. It's a long time to wait . . .'.

'Well, it doesn't have to be him. We would like to see any of the older men in the village.' I spoke rather impatiently as I looked at her narrow eyes clogged with matter. Then there was the sound of a movement in the room.

'What is it?' An old man, short in height, came out of the room and gave a light cough. He must have been lying in bed until then. At first glance his colour suggested he was not well, but his forehead, with the deep furrows of an old countryman who has toiled on the land all his life, showed that he was still healthy and the sharp eyes that shot a glance at me were quite powerful. First, I told him who we were, members of an army unit on a field training that had started a few days ago at the foot of the hill not far from the village.

'The thing is that during the morning while we were digging a trench we happened to find some human bones.'

'Bones?' He jerked up his head. At these words the woman who had remained on the floor shifted her bottom and tried to get to her feet.

'Yes, sir. They were unmistakably human. If we had known about it we would never have put a spade there in the first place, would we? It was such level ground, no one could have thought it was a grave. It didn't seem as if there were any other graves nearby.'

'Umn. I understand . . .'. It had been quite unexpected but the old man, as if he had known about it, slowly nodded his head.

'Whereabouts was it, Mr Soldierman?' asked the old woman as she strode across the wooden verandah. It was rather an unexpected reaction from her. While I was explaining to her roughly where it was, Private Oh stood by with his face in contortions. It was understandable, for he was the very one who had turned up with the tip of his spade the first piece of bone.

For the last few days we had been busy preparing the camp for the exercise. Today we had formed teams of two to dig defensive trenches a distance of two metres apart. The area allocated to our platoon was the third ridge of the hills. It so happened that Private Oh and myself took up a position on the left-hand side. The spot, which the platoon leader had marked for us by turning a circle on his heel, seemed somewhat flatter than its neighbourhood. It could have been a vegetable plot that had gone neglected for many years. As we stood by it we noticed that it was very thickly overgrown. Tough weeds like mugwort and thistles with dried-up leaves still hanging on to the stems stood in a solid tangle.

'Bloody hell,' said Oh. 'How sinister it looks – as if something is lurking there.' He wrinkled his nose to show his unwillingness, and I also felt uneasy myself as I looked down at the unpleasant mass of growth. Using our spades sideways we began by slashing the weeds at the bottom of their stems. They were so thick, they needed striking three or four times before they fell. It was fortunate that the surface of the earth was not frozen too hard. When we were knee-deep, we noticed the soil was now vividly different in colour from what it had been, more moist and dark red in colour. It was at about the same time that a sort of sour and mouldy smell seemed to well up from some unidentifiable source. It brought back to me the memory of the mouldy smell rising from the space underneath the verandah of the old house where I had lived as a child. It used to waft up gently on days when it looked as if there would be a downpour of rain. When I was alone in that big house with so much space, or when I was bored, I would lie on my stomach on the wooden floor, push my head over the edge of it and look into the space below. At the far end of it a darkness crouched. The incalculable depth of this eerie darkness and the mouldy smell that constantly wafted up roused a sharp pleasure and excitement that ran through me along with a quiet yet seductive fear as if I was witnessing in hiding the scene of a crime.

'Good heavens! What's this?' As we continued with our task even while we were sniffing, the private gave a shriek of urgency. When he had peered at the lump of earth that had come up on his shovel he flung it down and clambered out of the trench. In this confusion the bulk of what seemed to be a heavy lump of soil fell on my toes. It was a human skull. Two black holes that must once have held eyes shot me a look from amongst the earth. My colleagues came running and in a short space of time even the platoon leader and the adjutant had joined the spectators. The leader told us just to put it back in its place and to cover it over as it had been. Then the adjutant, Mr Kim, stepped forward as he waved his hand.

'You don't seem to understand, sir. Even though it may be the remains of a nameless person, it belongs to one of our forefathers. You can't treat it without due respect. It may seem a chance occurrence but, if you think about it it may be that it has happened in this way through some bond of fate, you never know. If we are not careful we may be turning our blessings into misfortunes.'

He said that he had experienced similar cases twice in the past and told us at length how badly things had turned out after he carelessly threw away even pieces of bones that were rolling about. He went on talking about several disasters that he said had really happened, even though they sounded incredible. He was the sort of chap who when bored would get hold of anyone and offer to tell their fortune by examining their palms.

In the end we carefully dug up the pieces of bone which had been buried without even a coffin. They were fairly well-preserved. Even though they had lain underground only knee-deep, they were incredibly orderly. The sour smell continued to rise from all around. We got the top part out first and proceeded to the torso.

'Good heavens!' When the latter part was lifted out those of us watching the process made some low exclamations.

'That's *beepee* wire, isn't it?', someone said as he pointed at the body. Wound round the thin bones of the ribs we saw several layers of wire. It was known as '*beepee* wire', still used by the army for telephones. We also saw the forearms and the wrists were tightly bound with it. Where the body had lain the earth was of an unusually dark red clay.

Standing by the pit keeping watch on what was going on I suddenly dropped my spade, unaware of myself, and it slide over the edge and fell in. I cannot tell how it happened, but the moment I saw those coils of thin wire bound round the body, all of a sudden I saw the wrinkled face of my mother. Leaning against a corner of the fence she mumbled to herself as she stared into the sky, 'Look at them. Even birds know how to return to their old home when the right time comes.'

'Don't you see, dear? What did I say? I saw him in my dream last night, I keep telling you.' The old woman spoke in a flustered tone.

'That's useless talk.'

'I mean it. He was just like he used to be. Smiling with that handsome face of his and he said he had come to see you. You know, it couldn't have been more realistic even if he had been in the flesh.'

'Stop it now. Why don't you go and get me a bottle of wine and some food? It seems they have found one of our elders. I can't just go empty handed, can I? . . .'. The old man, after abruptly dismissing her, went inside and came out again shortly wearing a dark grey overcoat. We slung our rifles over our shoulders and stood up. The old woman came out with a bottle of wine and wrapped up several dried pollack in some newspaper. We took them one each and tucked them under our arms.

'We are awfully sorry to cause you the trouble of going out in this cold,' I said.

'Not at all, young men. It is not necessarily other people's business . . .', he replied pleasantly as he lightly stepped over the threshold. The woman followed us as far as the village entrance.

'Please examine him carefully, dear. He was tall, and sturdily built. Of course you may recognize him. It was obvious that she did not mean to go any further. She stopped there as she gave him the instructions. He responded to her only with a nod of his head as he started to walk before us. It was only then that I noticed his limp. At a quick glance one might not have noticed it but now I saw clearly that as he walked he swayed from side to side. But his steps were regular. As we passed the lonely house, the mongrel came out and started barking as before. Perhaps he was not being fed enough. The skin of his belly stuck to his back and his bones were bulging as he showed off how well he could growl. The three of us walked on without a word along the line of telegraph posts that stood tall and exposed to the rain and wind amidst the plantations and fields. After a while I looked back and saw the old woman just turning round to walk homewards with her back bent.

I had seen my mother staring into the sky every autumn when the migrating birds came flying. But it was not until I was quite old that I understood why the migration of such insignificant birds made her eyes look so dreamy and soft, nor did I know why what was just a natural instinct for the birds as they sensed the change of season even before humans did and came south towards the warmer climate had such special meaning to her. It was one day about this time, as I was looking up at the birds as they flew over our village leaving behind the strange honking of their cries, that it dawned on me that she was probably waiting for someone. Once that occurred to me I noticed other things anew. In the midst of hoeing the furrows of the plantation under the fierce midsummer sun, she would often lift her head and stare endlessly at the point where the road stretched over the brow of the hill, her eyes dreamy and vacant. Sometimes while she was putting the washing on the line or trimming vegetables in the corner of the yard, she would cast her watery stare into the air as if momentarily her spirit had deserted her, and suddenly release a deep sigh. I must have been about twelve or so. It was also the time when I first realized and questioned the fact that there were just the two of us, my mother and myself.

'Your father is dead,' she told me when I asked about him. 'He went far away in a ship and never came back.' Then one day about that time when I became a high school boy, I came home alone, leaving my satchel in the classroom, ready to burst into tears. By chance I had heard from a classmate who was a distant relative an amazing secret about my father. I burst through the gates, ran into the house, grabbed my mother as if I would attack her and began to question her. I cannot even today forget the sad painful look that briefly passed over her face. She was careful to put on a calm face as she simply answered my questions.

'That's right. Your father had committed a crime. You are too young to understand this now. He had to leave home because of that. But,' she added, '. . . he had the most beautiful eyes. The only college student in the whole village . . . when his friends tried to harm some of the others he did all he could to stop them. There are quite a few who survived only thanks to him. It is true.'

Such excuses as she could make were hardly enough to be of any comfort to me. After this I rarely brought up the subject, probably because her words, admitting his crime so readily, were contrary to my expectations and left me with deep sense of shock. From that time on I developed a feeling that I had a share in my father's so-called crime, a burden I voluntarily took upon myself. And because of that I was growing into a child with eyes too serious for my age and acquiring a look of gloom.

From then on the dreaded visage of my father followed by my side like a curse. It always lurked behind me in the darkness as it shot glances at me with its infinitely sinister eyes. In fact he was hiding everywhere: in the blackness that crouched at the far end of the space underneath the wooden verandah of our house into which I often looked as I lay on my stomach and hung my head down over the edge; in the mouldy smell that issued gently from it, the man whose face I had never once seen would stare at me, his blood-shot eyes flashing. Like a stain of blood that you contracted from you know not where, that you could never remove even after a long time had passed, it had been stamped deep in me as a kind of curse and fear. Bearing this stigma in my breast, I could never escape from the great sense of guilt and the ominous sentiment that draped around me.

The wind that had been winding through the village came to spray an eerie chill, and still it blew. The old man steadily maintained his position in front of us. He was limping but his body was straight. To hold it up while limping must doubtless have been a strain. Probably the life he has lived, I thought to myself, may also have been a tough and strenuous one. On the distant slope I could see now and again the flocks of crows as they flew up and then landed again, their wings flapping. Each time they rose I had the illusion that one side of the sky was wavering and swelling like the body of a decaying animal.

'Don't you think, sir, we must have desecrated a grave belonging to that old man?' Private Oh crept close as he spoke.

'I don't think so. It couldn't have been a proper grave. Without even a coffin and in that unsightly manner . . .'.

'You may be right . . .'. He gave a wry smile as he shifted the weight of the bottle of wine from one side to the other.

'Huh, it looks like snow.' At the old man's voice from ahead I looked up. Indeed, there were dark clouds rising thickly at one end of the sky. Meantime the sun had disappeared. We were approaching the camp. When we had walked up the last part of the steep slope, the sergeant was ready to receive the old man. Having more or less finished digging the trenches, they had gathered wood, made a camp-fire and were warming their hands. Perhaps because of the unfamiliar atmosphere he looked rather embarrassed.

'We are very sorry, sir, to bring you out this far,' said the platoon leader, still with a boyish face, as he raised his hand in a salute to which the old man responded by bowing from the waist, rather confused.

We led him to where the remains were. The digging had been suspended from the time when we had left, but the bones in question had been gathered and laid out on some newspaper. He looked down at them with a blank expression for a long time and suddenly clicked his tongue. His wrinkled forehead looked gloomy.

'I was the one who gave the order to dig at this spot, I am sorry to say, but in the first place it didn't look at all like a grave. I can't understand how anyone could have been buried here,' said the platoon leader as if to justify himself, apprehensive that he might have made a blunder.

'If you knew the circumstances it wouldn't be at all unexpected,' said the man after a long silence as he stared down at the bones. 'This neighbourhood is that sort of a place.'

'So, it was as we had guessed? It happened during the war?'

'Not only here. You're likely to come across nameless bones like this if you dig anywhere within ten *li* of the village.'

'Was it as bad as that? I don't seem to remember hearing of any serious battles in this area.'

The old man cast a quick glance at the leader's youthful face which showed a suddenly whetted curiosity and turned round to gaze briefly at the distant mountains. 'This can't be the only village, I know, but we here have uniquely witnessed so many deaths that we became sick with the loathing of it. Look, over there.' He raised his arm to point at the mountains. There lay writhing the giant features of the Taibaik Mountain range, known as the backbone of the Korean peninsula, blocking out one end of the sky. We saw we were surrounded on all four sides with steep mountains that cut off our view. In whichever direction you ran to, it was obvious, you would soon be confronted by the sheer rise of a mountain face.

'That is the very backbone of the Taibaik range. Get on to it and follow the ridge lines, and they say it's one straight path from Chiri Mountain in the South to the Diamond Mountain in the North. In the olden days it was so thick with trees you couldn't see the sky.' We moved our gaze to follow the tip of his finger. The ridge line writhing like the back of a giant reptile ran straight towards a mountain to the north. We were told that it was surrounded by precipitous rockfaces like a folding screen, impossible for anyone to climb. So when they were forced to go round the long way, inevitably they went through the fields round this village. That had been the crux of the matter, he said. When the war was about to end, strangers began to flow in. A community that had hardly heard the sound of a gun when the war front was actually pushing past them on its way to the south now suddenly became a scene of carnage. People from the hills came down, mainly at night, to take away food and clothes. Sometimes they dragged village people away to be their guides. There were some groups said to have walked all the way from Mt Chiri. Thoroughly famished and worn out, they were on the run to the north. Eventually the Southern Army arrived to block their retreat and from then on the battle went on intermittently by day and night.

'In the end, we had an evacuation order so we had to go, but during this time of turmoil our number had greatly diminished.'

He went on to say that on the morning that followed a night disturbed by gunfire, they had to face the task of gathering and burying the dead, scattered white over the slopes of the hills. The war ended and the people came back. On the places where they had buried the bodies of strangers of whom they knew neither their origins nor their names, weeds thrived and grew every year as high as a man. Because of this, the old man said, for several years no one ventured to grow any root vegetables like potatoes or mooli.

Someone brought along an old towel and some more newspaper. The old man started to wipe the soil off the bones one by one with the towel and arrange them neatly on the paper.

'If that's what happened, this chap would have been a Red, wouldn't he?' The platoon leader said this as he pointed at the remains with his baton, the end of it bobbing up and down. The adjutant asked, 'Why do you think so?'

'You've just heard, haven't you, that many Red partisans were killed. This chap doesn't look as if he was a regular soldier and if he had been a member of the community his family wouldn't have left him like this, would they?'

'You can never tell. It was a time when both sides were killing and being killed . . .'.

At that moment the old man squatting as he carried on working with his hands spoke abruptly. 'Why for heaven's sake . . . what on earth does it matter? Even when they are dead – dead and lying like this – do you have to fuss about whether they belonged to one side or the other? What do the dead care? . . . it's all senseless. Tch! tch!'.

His voice was low but strong and powerful. Even while he talked his head was bent down as he meticulously wiped the mud off the bones. He manœuvred his hands with great care as if he was dealing with precious objects, showing no signs of haste, and we stood around him and watched over his small body. We kept our mouths shut for a long time and I noticed his fingers damp from the soil were trembling slightly.

'Should we, the living, disturb the sleep of the dead? We mustn't. These sorrowful departed ones should be helped to lie in peace even in their death. That's the obligation of us, the living . . . but look how he has been tied up, what an uncomfortable sleep he must have had.' His tone of voice had changed to one of rebuke as he mumbled to himself. After meticulously rubbing the dirt from the skull and the leg bones, he began to untie the wire round the torso. The tight knots finally came loose from the pressure of his finger tips. The steel wire was as good as new. It could ring with a sharp metallic sound even now. The thought of its amazing endurance and cold inhumanity in resisting to the end the long period of time and the darkness underground that had melted away the flesh and even rusted the bones suddenly made me shudder.

When he had undone and loosened the wire that had been tied round the arms and the wrists he straightened his back, rose to his feet and walked a little way back taking the bundle of the wire with him. At the moment when he hurled it away into the air I saw, for no reason, the thin neck of my mother as she stood in the courtyard looking into the sky, and the white porcelain bowl of water that she used to put on a small table every morning appeared before my eyes and then vanished. I lit a cigarette and brought it to my lips. In the far distance, the desolate hills of early winter lay as if dead, revealing their bare backs. I felt giddy.

My mother with a basket on her head was walking along the sandy shore of the river towards me, coming alone from the opposite direction to the bubbling sound of the flowing water. The sand shone silver as it reflected the sunlight. She had a cloth belt bound tightly round her waist and the ends of her skirt fluttered lightly in the breeze. My eyes narrowed against the brilliance of the sun. I was watching her constantly. Then it happened. As if in a dream I saw the figure of a man following her closely. It was my father. Unmistakably it was the man I had seen in the framed picture that I had found some time ago hidden deep beneath the clothes in her worn chest of drawers, the man in a student's uniform. The man that was said to have left me behind in my mother's womb and gone in a great hurry following mountain paths towards Mt Chiri or some such place, a man with pale cheeks, scantily built, was walking home with my mother. With wondering eyes I was sitting on the grass as I watched them approach. When at last she was close enough for me to see clearly her eyebrows, nose, the outline of her lips and even her thin, emaciated neck, the image of the man had gone, like magic. I rubbed my eyes several times and looked again but it was no use. On the white, sparkling sandy beach were only her footprints that doggedly followed her heels like a ghost.

With no coffin, we enclosed the remains in newspapers and put them back where they had been. When we had covered the globular mound of the grave with turf we felt as if we had carried out at least the minimum formalities. The old man poured a little wine over it. Then after taking a mouthful of it himself he passed the cup round. Private Oh put out the dried fish the old woman had given him and thanks to what had happened we were having an unexpected drinking party.

'Well, this out-of-the-blue funeral feast is thanks to you two. Come on and have a cup each.'

'Hear, hear. Anyway you've done a good deed so you can count on a place in heaven.' The platoon leader tilted the bottle and the others added their comments as they chuckled. I lifted the full cup in both hands.

'Look at that! Even the flying creatures know how to come

home when the time is right,' I heard my mother saying. A stranger stood a little way away. His body and arms bound with wire, he was staring this way, slightly bent forward. His sunken eyes were filled with fear. The reports of a gun rang out and he was falling forward. My vision suddenly became blurred.

Ah, my father! Where is he lying now? Sending forth each year mugwort and thistles to thrive in abundance over his head, would he be lying beneath deserted furrows or at the shady foot of a hill with neither grave nor stone, sleeping alone? The wine was dripping from my cup.

I was coming down the slope with the old man. He waved his hand several times trying to persuade me to go back. Reversing the order this time I was in the lead. Dark grey clouds were gathering low. As if chased by the wind they were swirling wildly as they scurried from the ridges of the hills opposite.

Once on the main road we walked abreast. Dragging his foot on one side his pace was slower than before. Now and again the wind swirling behind us lifted up the ends of his long *durumaggi*.

'Excuse me, sir, for asking, but overhearing what your wife said earlier on gave me the impression that you were looking for somebody.' I asked because I remembered her telling him to look closely at the remains, but he just walked on without a word. I was beginning to wonder whether I had brought up the wrong subject when he spoke.

'To tell you the truth, I lost my elder brother at that time and also my leg has been like this since then. He was dragged away in the middle of the night as a guide. Hearing a rumour that he had been shot along with his captors I ran out and searched everywhere but for some reason I failed to find his body.'

We were already turning off on to the narrow road that led to the village. 'Then, today, my wife says she saw him in her dream last night. Silly woman . . . perhaps it was an omen of what was to happen today.' I was feeling strange as I remembered Private Oh talking about his dream. 'Do you reckon the remains you saw were perhaps . . .'.

'Well, how can anyone recognize anything at this stage? Unless there are some particular features . . . Whoever it may have been we have helped one poor soul by settling him comfortably – though belatedly – underground. Wasn't that a good thing to happen?' He laughed forlornly. The wind rose at that moment and swallowed up the sound. Suddenly, I felt it was dark. As I looked in the direction from which the wind blew, the other side across the plain looked blurred as if seen through frosted glass.

'Snow is on the way. The first snow of the year, isn't it?'

'Yes, I think so.'

For a long time we stood together at the edge of the field gazing without words as snowflakes began to fall and turn the ground whitish. Across the fields I could see the roofs of the village. Probably they were cooking supper. A few strands of thin smoke rose and thinned out like the unravelling of a skein of wool.

'I am nearly there now. You must go back. It's a long way for you to go on your own.' He smiled as he gestured with his hand. I obediently stopped. In no time he was some distance away, lurching with each step. Amidst the snowflakes, growing bigger, his back, as it receded, looked singularly forlorn. I stood there and watched him until his form went completely out of sight behind the curving edge of the field.

No sooner had I heard the sound of the meal table being put down over my head than my mother shook me to wake me up. It was the day after I had arrived home on my first leave from the army. After travelling all day on a slow train I had collapsed and fallen into a deep sleep the moment I set foot in the house. I got up rubbing my eyes, and was surprised to see a full array of food on the table. My mother gave me a shy smile like that of a child as she looked at me.

'You won't believe it but I was so taken up with the thought of your coming home that I completely forgot. It turns out to be his birthday.'

'Who do you mean?'

'Your father, of course.' Having said this excitedly, she started and was embarrassed as she examined my expression. My heart sank with a bump. 'Are you mad or something, mother? I've asked you never to bring up that subject again, haven't I? He's been dead long since. Even if, by any chance he was alive somewhere it would be a hundred times better for us for him to be dead.'

'Don't speak like that, child. He might still be alive, you never know.'

'He's dead. Accept that as a fact!'

'I can't . . . If only he's alive somewhere, it's possible someday we might meet him again . . .'.

At last I exploded. 'How? How should we meet him at this

stage? In what sort of way could we meet him, tell me that!' I spat out the words as they came to me. My hand holding the spoon was almost shaking.

'Oh, no. I am sorry. How stupid, I am . . . this stupid mouth of mine causes nothing but trouble.' She quickly turned with her back to me. And hurriedly lifted the front end of her jacket to her eyes. She was crying. She had hardly ever shown tears in front of me, her only son, before. The woman who, even when she was ill in bed, would press her lips tightly and try to show that she was all right, was now letting her tears flow freely.

Ah, how completely had I forgotten that she had been waiting for someone for such a long time. The eyes of a man that had stared at me in my childhood in the darkness underneath the wooden floor amidst the rising damp and unpleasant smell, the name of that hateful man that had remained as a deep wound scorching black my heart even now when I was a grown up – the hateful name of this man my mother had been cherishing secretly and alone in her heart like a seed of fire all these twenty-five years. In fact, this man could have had little substance for her except for his beautiful and caring eyes and the gentle voice that remained with her always.

Probably it was not only because of her perverse waiting, almost obstinacy, that she was crying. Indeed, she must have known better than anyone how her waiting was being pushed back further and further beyond her grasp. A time-span of twenty-five years and the obstinate self-deception that had been binding her up to now throttled her neck and so she was weeping without restraint. With the meal table in front of me I sat with my head drooping. All I saw were the dark strands of the seaweed, a birthday food, like the long dark passage of our family, growing cold in the soup bowl.

The features of the old man were no longer in sight. Treading the snow that was by now quite deep I slowly retraced my way. At each step the rifle on my shoulder clashed with the water flask and gave out a clanging sound. I was again keenly aware of the offensive feel of the metal and the exact weight of it. I thought about the nature of its muzzle, always open, aiming at someone and the depth of the frightful darkness inside the small round hole crouching with an absolute firmness.

'Caw, caw.' Whenever they had come, there was a great crowd of crows squirming about among the furrows. In the abundance of snow that was falling and piling up all around, these creatures gathered exclusively in their own kind, wriggling, black, diffused a sinister and ominous air like an epidemic. Suddenly I heard amidst the falling flakes of snow the sound as of someone lying beneath the frozen ground, curled like a shrimp, turning over. It was my father. His hands and feet were bound up and he was issuing forth low moans as now and again he turned over. Standing in the middle of the desolate field I watched for a long long time the flapping wings and wriggling movements of the big ominous birds.

Above my head the snow fell constantly in gigantic petals. As if set to fill up the whole world with its large and lovely flakes it was effacing the lines of the furrows, the paths amongst the field, my ankles that stood on it, the wriggling forms of the black birds and eventually even the outlines of the great mountains opposite in white, all white. It was a brilliant whiteness that made you narrow your eyes – the very whiteness of the porcelain bowl which my mother used to fill with the fresh water she had fetched from the well and put on a small table at the dawn of each day.

# A THIN LINE

## Yoo Keumho

LOOKING at the picture, I felt an eerie chill rising within me. The background was predominantly red on which was set a blue bird.

'It was done by and elderly shaman,' said the professor. He added, 'Through pictures of flying birds or butterflies they can take flight into a world of fantasy. The more they are cramped within the walls of the real world the richer and wilder grows their imagination.'

Shaman customs was a branch of Folklore Studies. Feeling a sort of distaste for this kind of research, in which Professor Paik, a friend since our high school days, was deeply involved, I often spoke harshly of it – 'It's a queer subject for a so-called university professor to be making a living out of, isn't it?'

Regardless of my scoffing remarks, he went on, 'You'd be interested to know that these people, without exception, become shamans, not from their own voluntary choice, but more because they have been led by the nose in mysterious and incomprehensible ways. They remain bound by strong ties to that world until they die . . . Why, don't you like these pictures? I was going to mount a couple of them and make you a present of them . . . ha, ha, ha . . .'.

'For heaven's sake, don't spoil my drink.'

The ten or more pictures apparently by shamans that he spread out before me were, without exception, connected with images of butterflies, birds, flowers and light. Especially the colour of red, which was the dominant tone, reminiscent of a vivid sunset, made me cringe.

The sunset colours, in a weird sort of way, brought back to me the colour in the eyes of my father when he used to stare at us from the time he came back as a wounded soldier until the day he drew his last breath, and the colour in the eyes of the shaman from the mountain who often came to see my mother on the pretext of praying for a long life for my father, and also the contorted face of the man with a bushy beard who lived behind us in a house that had been freely ventilated by bullets.

'Come on, drink up.' I would say, 'I haven't the slightest interest in your studies, I can tell you.' Nevertheless, whenever we were together he would talk about shaman customs and, unaware of myself, I must have occasionally joined in.

'On a chilly day, after bathing in cold water, a woman wriggles and writhes on the floor of the shrine like the coiling of a snake . . . that scene you stealthily peeped on as a boy, that was an actual scene of sexual intercourse with God experienced in fantasy. Once she has invoked a spirit to possess her, a shaman avoids, in principle, all worldly sex . . .'.

'Can't you for once stop talking about ghosts? It takes away my appetite.'

I hardly ever speak to anyone about my childhood. I never had until, probably in a state of intoxication, I must have told him about the shaman that once lived in our village. He said, 'I mean that girl – you said her name was Gudnim, I think. Didn't you say she had been adopted by a shaman?'

'For goodness' sake, can't you ever cure your nasty habit of digging away at little details?'

'It's a name that slipped out of your own mouth once when you were drunk, so there.'

'Damn you!'

'Didn't you know that a man who's as fond of alcohol as you are has a natural tendency to shamanism? Escaping reality in a drunken stupor and immersing oneself in a world of fantasy, as they do, are basically the same thing, you see.'

'Very clever.'

'I also see latent shamanism in a woman undergoing a surgical operation to make her eyelids double-folded. According to my statistics, there's no shaman whose eyes are not large and with double-folded lids. Look at this young lady here . . .'. He pointed at the waitress, serving the drinks, who had double-folded eyes and who gave him a sharp look. My meetings with him always went like this.

I had not seen him for some time. During this period there had been a couple of occasions when the shaman's pictures he had shown me came back to me. But only in momentary, passing thoughts. I had been so deeply absorbed in my work at the office that he had almost gone out of my mind.

Then this fishing party – that was to blame. Although having not the slightest interest I had been lured by my colleagues at work into joining them on this trip, and one morning we had set off. When, at the journey's end, in a country village densely wrapped in fog on top of the rain, I saw the professor waving to me and chuckling, I momentarily flinched at the fancy that perhaps I had been hooked on a line that he had cast.

To make everything even more fantastic, all around was pear blossom. Pathetically sodden by the rain, pale blue, like the face of a shaman in a trance, they were in full bloom all over the place, in the fields and over the vegetable plots.

Probably it was only because of the few white strands that I had discovered in my hair as I looked into the mirror a few days before that I had agreed to go on that angling party. When I stepped out into the alleyway at the dawn of that day, how strangely unfamiliar was the sight of the city lying still in the darkness. My own footsteps echoed loudly and the main road, usually so heavy with traffic that it throws you off balance, was like a silted shore at low tide.

'White hairs. They've arrived.' A streak of sadness, like a thin rivulet, was flowing across my heart. In the unfamiliarity of the city and the cool, refreshing darkness, I was nursing a sentiment that melted strangely within me like a sweet on one's mouth. The fog, mingling with the darkness of the dawn, made the air damp and sticky. Carried away by the fancy that this damp and sticky darkness was dragging me into some deep abyss, I heard my colleagues chattering as if in a dream.

'Spring fishes gather among water weeds.' 'Last time, Mr Kim caught one, one metre seventy long, didn't he? That rightly deserved the prize, so why didn't he get it?'

'Huh, huh. It's just as well the hook was in its lip. If it had been in the eye, well, well . . . it's not likely that he had a daughter like Sim Chong, the one in the fairy tale . . .'.

'Mr Chang. You've come empty-handed, haven't you?'

Only at this point did I come out of my reverie and accept a cigarette offered by a colleague. 'I have a plenty of rods, so don't you worry,' he said. 'Who knows? On your first attempt, you might catch one over a foot. Then you will be bothering me to take you out fishing every week, won't you?'

'I have been too deeply engrossed in my work. Look, my hair is turning white,' I said.

By the time the minibus had got through the city centre, raindrops were beginning to spatter. Well equipped with things like raincoats and gumboots, my friends did not seem to pay much attention to it. As the drops became bigger I began to wonder whether I would have been better off at home.

'It's not just about catching fish . . . drinks, and time can be caught as well . . . ha, ha . . .'.

'Fish bite better on cloudy days, actually.' My friends were still quite optimistic even when it started to rain, a fine spray more like fog. By the time we were completely out of the city, had turned on to a country road, and saw the breakfast smoke rising from village chimneys, it became obvious that the rain now coming in thick streaks was not likely to stop.

'A true fisherman makes a killing on a day like this. You see, the carp. . . .' Even now someone was bragging.

As the streaks of the rain became heavier, the fog seemed to lift a little. Outside, thanks to the rain, the fresh green stood out even more vividly and I was beginning to enjoy myself. A look-out hut on stilts left from the previous year with only its frame remaining, houses along the road that had been transformed into an imitation of western style, cow and its calf standing by the corner of one of them, the vinyl greenhouses, one after another, a big farm bordered by acacia trees, and the pear trees just bursting into bloom.

'Look, there's a shaman shrine!' one of us shouted as he slid open the window. 'Amazing in this age and time!' We passed an ancient beech tree, its thick trunk draped and hung with colourful pieces of cloth. At its foot was a pile of stones.

'If you have a wish, you can go and make it there.'

'All I want is to catch big fish – over a foot – ten of them'll do, ha, ha . . .'.

Carried away with life in Seoul – more than five cups of coffee a day, the constant ringing of the telephone and the looks of boredom as we ask each other each day at the same hour, 'What shall we have for lunch today?' – for a long time I had quite forgotten the walls of mud bricks, the pail by the water well and the black and white smoke when you snap the green branches of pine trees and try to burn them . . .

'You won't come back with fish from the market, will you, darling?' my wife had said as she turned over to go back to sleep. On her dressing table was an array of cosmetic jars and electronic gadgets the purpose of which I didn't have the foggiest idea.

After leaving the asphalt road, the wheels of our bus became stuck in the mud at least twice and each time we had to get out and push. We went over a slope on which stood a derelict hut which used to house a communal funeral bier. When the bus at last stopped by a small reservoir, I found myself moved deeply by a strange emotion. There, incredibly, were laid out about a dozen traditional thatched cottages. How similar it was to the village where I had lived as a boy! The cowsheds, large iron cauldrons for boiling the feed, the fenceless hut of mud bricks, its rafters scorched by the smoke from the chimney . . . They were there as a reminder of some painful memories. I felt a kind of uncomfortable embarrassment as if the bus had been somehow travelling backwards in time through the five, fifteen, twenty years and then suddenly dropped me there.

It was here that later, in the day, I was to meet Professor Paik. He had told me that he searched every nook and cranny of the land for his material and that there was hardly a spot that his feet had not trodden. Even so I was quite unprepared to see him here.

As soon as they had put their baggage down in the rented rooms of a small cottage by the reservoir my colleagues ran off to the water, each seeking his own vantage spot, in the way baby spiders scatter and disappear.

'Don't you like fishing, Mr Yoon?' I asked as I realized there was another man beside me who could not be bothered to brave the rain – the elderly caretaker at work.

'What would I want those little fish for? Ha, ha, ha . . . besides, there is wine to be drunk . . .'.

One end of the verandah was piled with long bundles of dry grass, and over the shoulder of the woman who was feeding the fire in the *ondol* stove I could see lettuces thriving in a small plot by the house.

'Look at those pear blossoms,' said Mr Yoon. 'They are terrible

– make you sad.' Here and there, on the *ondol* floor, pasted over with old newspaper, rose wisps of smoke leaking from below. 'I love this smell of burning, don't you?' he said. 'You feel the floor getting warm so quickly . . . We all know, sir, that you enjoy a drink . . . of course we do, ha, ha . . .'. Whisky did not seem to be the right sort of drink for a place like this, but he fetched from the baggage a bottle of whisky and some dry snacks.

'Is it getting warm?' The elderly matron of the house felt the floor with her hand, showing gnarled joints on the fingers.

'Oh, no. No thank you . . . I can't take this?' She waved her hand but nevertheless she firmly grasped the glass of whisky that he had poured out for her and slipped it down, saying, 'My goodness, this is not drink. It's more like fire.'

'Where is your home town, sir?'

'My home town?' I was gazing at the two old pear trees in the vegetable plot by the house. They were covered in blossom. Saturated by the rain, they were pathetic, almost bluish. He went on, 'My wife and a son and a daughter . . . in my home village, there were such a lot of pear trees . . . We got safely over the border, the thirty-eighth Parallel. It's all fate I suppose. There is no other way to explain it but to blame fate. By the time I reached Seoul, I was the only one left . . .'.

'So you are another one of those who were made homeless?'

'Well, for people like me, a home is where there is a warm bed and a full stomach, that's all . . .'. Two reddish rings appeared round his eyes.

My father was brought back after being injured twice in the front line. Full of anguish, he has passed away within less than a year of his homecoming. He had thrown away all our family fields and paddies, never very many, in his anguished drinking. How totally had I kept the past buried! Maybe, it was partly because his ashes had been scattered, according to his will. If there had been a grave, would I have visited the village of my origins at least occasionally? No! I would never have gone back whatever the circumstances.

The room, filled with the smoke of dry grass and the drone of the rain, was cosy. The repeated rhythm of the rain dripping from the eaves of a thatched roof, the wet walls of mud and stone and the murmur of Mr Yoon as he talked about his native village.

And behind his back in the plot by the house, the pear blossoms saturated by the rain were giving forth a bluish glow.

Even if he had a grave, I would never have visited it. I had consciously turned my back on my own village. How hard had I tried to forget that I had ever been a member of that community . . . I had been drinking continuously and I now felt quite intoxicated.

My father had returned to us with two crutches under his armpits in place of his left leg. It was a time when the Northern partisans who had fled to the hills still crept down into the village by night, and my father, after throwing away his leg in the Southern Army, had returned to the two of us, my mother and myself. But, in reality, it was not just his leg that he had lost. Between the time of his return and his death, his eyes were always inflamed and flashed wildly. He drank bottles of spirits one after the other. And once every three days he would grab the tress of mother's hair by the roots in an ingenious way and thrash her about in the courtyard as he screamed, 'Are you going to tell the truth or not? I must hear it from your own mouth, do you hear?'

His wooden crutch struck her countless times on shoulders, waist and legs while her arms twined round her head, she cried piteously, yet always mindful to keep the sound low.

'It's a world where people kill each other on any excuse. Tell me, how did you, the wife of a man in the Southern Army, survive in one piece? To which Red bastard did you open your legs to save your own dirty life? Tell me, tell me, do you hear?'

Sometimes it went on for fifteen or twenty minutes, or at the longest, half-an-hour. Eventually he would end up by weeping himself as he beat his single leg. Mother's low cries and those of father, as if he would choke, made a weird harmony, and about this time the sky in the west would take on the colour of blood. That weird struggle – one party being beaten, yet never trying to escape while the other flailed the crutch until he was exhausted, ending up with the two of them crying together in a duet of cries and grunts – came to a halt when one day father drank three bottles of spirits in quick succession and breathed his last.

The words that the men had uttered clicking their tongues dozens of times while they wrapped his body in the shroud had remained to me as a mystery for a long time.

'That of all things a bullet should've taken away his prick!'

'That was a shame.'

'Still, he has at least left behind a seed, and died inside his own home. That must count as a blessing with the world the way it is.'

I remember one particular occasion. That day, as usual, in a severe fit, he had struck my mother. She was hit on the head and two thin trails of blood trickled down. At that moment she raised her head briefly, just once. It looked bluish, and for the first time she did not cry. I don't know why such an idea came to me then but her expression reminded me of pear blossom, and, at the same time, of the colour of the shaman's face at the Sansin Shrine.

'Look! Blood, blood, blood . . .'. My father must have gone mad. He was uttering queer sounds as he caught it in his hands and rubbed it over his face as if he was washing in it. He gave a contorted smile and went on screaming incoherently.

Once I had left the village I tried to rub out, one by one, the fragments of any memories of my childhood. I crushed and buried them in the deepest darkness as matters that had nothing at all to do with me. From the time that I crept, with my mother, into a shanty town in Seoul, I never breathed a word to anyone about my home village or my parents. Even to my wife, I had never made any mention of them. As I left the village long ago I had floated them away on the waters of the valley in which it stood.

I am an orphan, I had said to myself. Like the legendary hero, Sonogong, I was from a stone. For everyday life one does not need the past. Life is too busy. Of course it is. It does not allow one the leisure to indulge in the memories of days gone by. Of course it doesn't. I had been a night school student, a temporary employee of a firm, a regular worker with a better one and then a section chief and now I had a responsible position in a first-rate company. In no way could I afford the time to revive old memories or think about the old village . . .

It had all started quite accidentally a few days ago. Looking into the mirror, and as I confirmed the swelling of my wife's belly, I became somewhat flustered.

'What's wrong with you?' she asked.

'Fix me a drink, can you?'

'That's not like you. You don't usually drink at home. What's this sudden change about?'

'It doesn't matter. There must be some whisky left somewhere.'

And I added that I wanted to go on a fishing trip. 'I feel rather tired.'

'You've gone very queer, darling, all of a sudden.'

'Pass me another drink, Mr Yoon, will you? It's certainly more agreeable to fish for whisky than for carp. Don't you think so?'

'Of course, I do, sir, but if the rain subsides a bit in the afternoon, wouldn't you like to try it just for a few minutes? Even the fish prefer the boss, you see.'

By the time the anglers rolled in they were all soaked through and blue-lipped. I had consumed a considerable quantity of the whisky.

'Ha, Mr Chang, do you really mean to fish for nothing but alcohol?'

'I am fishing for time actually, don't you see . . .'. Dinner was brought into the room, which was pungent with smoke seeping through the cracks in the floor. By the time several cups of wine had been drunk the keen anglers, nine out of the party of fifteen, had already disappeared again in the direction of the water. The remainder squatted at the warm end of the room each with a hand of cards.

'Look, my raincoat is hanging on the pillar, and my gumboots are over there,' said my colleague. He must have been thoroughly frozen by the rain. He sat on the warmest spot in the room and indicated the direction with his jaw. 'I bet you want to be able to say that at least you dipped a line into the water. After all, it is an angling party.'

'I shall have a go without any bait. That'll be some fishing, won't it?'

'Do as you like.'

As I threw this meaningless joke, I picked up a rod.

'Wait a minute, sir. You can't just . . .'. It was old Yoon who started fixing a worm on to the hook. Of course, I wouldn't have gone without it.

I went staggering down the slippery path between the paddies. I felt a shiver running down my spine. Raindrops drummed on the shoulders of my raincoat as if they were fragments of the time that was buried deep.

Whether it be a crucian or a carp . . . the beating of the rain made small wavelets on the surface of the water on which the red float kept bobbing.

With a tiny worm, no more than two centimetres, suspended beneath it, invisible to the angler himself . . . Suddenly I started giggling to myself. The moment of an encounter when through this thin strong cord two living things joined up in one – what kind of significance would that moment have? A hook that doggedly pulls one into itself not allowing you to escape. What is the meaning of that hook?

From the other side of the lake came a shout of 'It's a *wolchok*!'* as someone briskly lifted his rod. But the float on my line, trapped in the small wavelets made by the raindrops, kept on bobbing, neither going down nor coming up.

'Sir.' Suddenly, Yoon was holding an umbrella over my head. 'This girl has come to look for you.'

'For me?' A bob-haired girl of about twelve with a thoroughly rustic air gave a pale, bright smile, her blue lips chattering with cold.

'Who are you?'

'Gudnim.'

'Who?'

'Gudnim. That is my name, Pak Gudnim.'

I guessed that Professor Paik must be somewhere on the other side of the reservoir. It turned out that he was on a trip collecting material for his research when he saw the vehicle belonging to our company and he had sent a note to ask whether I was among the party.

'I am caught. I am properly hooked, ha ha, ha.' I mumbled to myself as I read his memo.

'Pardon?' said Yoon. He was checking my bait.

'I am hooked by the nose. Truly caught. Well, now you might as well try and catch a few yourself.'

I walked up the path between the paddies following the girl. 'At school they call me Malja, meaning the last child, but at home I'm Gudnim.' She flashed a smile and snuffled hard.

'I see. To tell you the truth, I had a girlfriend long, long ago. Her name was Gudnim. That's why I was so surprised.'

'Hee, hee . . .' the girl with bob-hair giggled freely as she walked in front of me.

'Tell me, where is the male shaman who sent this memo?'

'He's a teacher at a grand school. He's not a shaman.'

*A large specimen – over one foot in length.

'I bet he's a real shaman. So where is he?'

'At my house.'

'Your house?'

'He's been there for two days now. You see, tonight the shaman living below our place is going to lift the spirit of a man who was drowned when we had the big flood here sometime back.'

Professor Paik had come as far as where the bus was parked and he broke into a chuckle as he waved. 'A craving to go fishing is also one of the basic tendencies of shamanism. Ha, ha, ha . . . don't you think so? Lifting up a fish from the invisible depths of the water and lifting the spirit of a dead man . . . anyway it's good to see you. I know a place in the next village where they keep a wonderful home-brew.'

'You – the shaman ghost – you've come after me, haven't you . . . ha, ha . . .'.

The room, its walls smeared with the blood of housebugs, was just like the ones we used to have in our village.

'When I am in places like this, I feel so much at home,' said my friend. 'I am particularly happy this time because the heroine of the day is an extraordinary beauty. It is rare to come across such a dramatic opportunity. You are very lucky to be here too.'

'What? Have I caught a big one?'

The rustic home-brew blended with the whisky I had been drinking in the morning. 'Is it true that the child's name is Gudnim?'

'Why not?'

'Don't you think it a bit strange?'

'I understand the shaman's name is Gudnim too. It is fairly common, I think, for youngest daughters to be given names like that. Is there something on your mind?'

'Come off it. The tiresome habit of so-called scholars and teachers – digging into small details.'

If she had been alive, she would be about thirty-two or -three – the girl that used to live on the ridge of the hill . . .

'By the way' I put in, 'is there such a thing as a shaman who is not quite possessed by the spirit?'

'Yes. Occupational or hereditary shamans are the examples. People like that go so far as to deny the spirit itself while they carry out the ritual by rote . . .'.

After this I tried as far as possible to steer the conversation in a different direction. Nevertheless, I could not help feeling that like a fish unexpectedly hooked, suspended on a fine strong line, I was sinking little by little towards some mysterious destination. It was not entirely due to the alcohol. Was it perhaps because of the misty rain, a rain that sprayed like mist?

'I don't believe in anything, do you hear? Apart from the things that I can hold in my hand and feel on my tongue, I believe nothing. Does it sound as if I've fallen pretty low? I don't care. I don't believe in what happened yesterday, nor in the future unless it has some direct connection with present reality. What a load of rubbish I am talking . . .'.

Unlike my usual self I poured out these rather senseless, drunken ravings, even with gesticulations, to an old school friend, a fastidious scholar.

Because of the fog, the spot by the river where a crowd of people hummed looked like a lake quite separate from the river. The sound of the flute and cymbals became faster and faster and spread over the surface of the river to disappear into the fog. At last the moment came when the brass bowl that was supposed to scoop out the spirit of the dead man was thrown into the river from the shaman's hand. She chanted:

> '. . . forty-two-year-old Head of the Chung family, please come up.
>
> You are the one who mastered the Thousand Characters at the age of five and read *Rono* at seven.
>
> You, the Head of the Chung family, were known as a prodigy for a hundred miles in all directions.
>
> You were filial to your parents, loving to your brothers, doing village work as if it was your own.
>
> Have you forgotten your wife and children?
>
> How is it that you remain a forlorn spirit beneath the waters?
>
> How unbearably sad and regrettable.
>
> Come up here quickly and see the faces of your wife and children.
>
> Take a proper leave of them, and then you may go to an abode in Paradise . . .'.

The shaman's left hand holding the cord at the end of which the brass bowl was fastened began slowly to shake. The side of her pallid face reminded me of my mother when her head had been broken and run with blood, a long time ago.

'Don't you think she's beautiful?' Professor Paik whispered into my ear. The convulsion in her left hand was transmitted via the cord to the water and it began to be distorted by gentle waves on a surface that had been calm.

'. . . Come quickly, rise up and come over here, please do.
Your wife and children and the family are all in such anguish, soon there will be a pile of dead bodies.
Hurry up, do hurry up.
The eternal life in Paradise . . .'.

The sound of gong and cymbals quickened its tempo and the bell in her right hand tinkled loudly.

As the convulsions that had begun on her left wrist spread up to her shoulders and then to her whole body, her pallid face suddenly turned briefly in our direction.

Gudnim! At once I felt an eerie chill run through my whole body as I was caught in a hallucination.

'The spirit is coming up!'

'His spirit is rising!' Some of the spectators began to shout as the family of the man broke into keening. The din of bell, gong and cymbals. . . . In the fog that overlaid the river everything appeared milky and phantom-like, as in a dream.

'Look, it's coming! His spirit has come!'

By now I was grabbing hold of the bony hand of Professor Paik in sheer terror. A name tablet, tall as the span of a hand, carved out from chestnut wood, that was laid on the table with sacrificial food, was certainly moving in response to the convulsions that shook the shaman's whole body, and the fierce stare of her blood-shot eyes. At first I thought it was a hallucination, but there was no mistaking it. On a black-laquered, hexagonal table made of date wood, the tablet was jumping up and down.

Ah, ah! I could not breathe. Helpless with fright, I repeated inwardly 'It's Gudnim, it's certainly her.'

'Father . . . father' A girl of about fifteen, probably the dead man's daughter, started calling and sobbing as she beat her palm on the sandy beach. The sorceress, following the cord that passed through her hands, took one step after another into the water.

Gudnim!

I was telling myself, now she is fishing for her lost childhood.

In the water that laps her ankles and then her shins, in each wavelet, she is taking away the crust of time past, jumping across the twenty-odd years, as she slowly sinks back into her girlhood days in a black hemp skirt, when she was hungry, her shins smeared with dirt, while sniffling through her runny nose.

I recalled a particular day of her childhood, the day on which she had picked up a half-rotten sweet potato from the pigswill in our backyard. When she felt my eyes looking, embarrassed and frightened, she tried to escape, moving backwards, one step at a time, her face turning white. When she could go no further, blocked by the steep side of the hill, she looked up at me, her huge eyes trembling. . . . Her forehead was covered in downy hair and her eyelashes were very dark. Suddenly I thrust into her hand a piece of steamed rice-cake which she held uncomprehending for a moment, and then her eyes filled with tears.

'It's all right,' I said. 'I know all about how your father was killed by the people from the mountains, and your mother dragged away . . . so the shaman of the Sansin Shrine has taken you in . . .'. As the moisture that filled her eyes hung in tiny drops on her lashes, I wondered how the rays of the setting sun had got, in pieces, into those drops. Now she was eating the cake ecstatically in big bites until only half was left. Then she warily looked about. The sun that had stayed in the drops hanging from her lashes neatly slipped behind the ridge of Soori Mountain and suddenly it seemed that the red of the sky had got into her eyes. They began to burn little by little.

'I am so frightened of the old witch,' she said. All around was quiet. Only the bamboo leaves rustled as they brushed against one another. The sunset had not only entered her eyes but spread over her cheeks, now crimson.

'I mean . . . I can'. She stuttered between swallowing hard as her hand holding the cake swiftly lifted her black hemp skirt. 'I can keep it secret from Kiljoo.'

As I stood nonplussed she held my hand with her other hand and led it through the elasticated top of her drawers. As far as I can remember it was the first time that I had seen a smile that showed her white teeth.

'It's all right. I will keep it secret from Kiljoo.'

I took out my hand and ran hard along the path between vegetable plots, the sound of the lashing wind whirring till I felt as if I would collapse.

'The cruel bastards did it to Gudnim, the poor little lamb . . . May heaven strike them, the cowards worse than the animals . . .'. Here my memories become confused. I am not sure just when I came to understand the meaning of this gossip passed to my mother by an elderly neighbour. It could be at some point long after the war had ended, when the awareness came to me that I could well have been the first to have touched the small dry sex of this emaciated little creature. Or it may be that I gathered that she had been assaulted from what I overheard the village elders talking among themselves with clicking of tongues, as they were laying out the corpse of my father.

'When you think about it, this so-called "science" is quite absurd. The wider becomes the scope of scientific conquests – the spaceship *Columbia* has been out there and back – the deeper the mystery, what we may call the realm of the gods, grows. Do you see what I mean?'

The sounds of weeping and the bell swaddled in the fog seemed to draw the space in which we were standing into some time deep in the past.

'It is rarely that anyone voluntarily wants to become a shaman. So how is it that nevertheless they are being produced? The further science develops, I am inclined to say, the deeper grows the abyss of mystery on the opposite side.'

The fog began to thicken over the shore.

'Those professionals who became shamans simply to inherit a family tradition or because they have grown up as the adopted daughters of a shaman, all refrain from sexual intercourse with ordinary men. They detest it. Of course the case of those who really believe they are possessed is different as they indulge in sex with the spirit in their fantasy. Why do you think the ones who are not possessed still abhor it?'

'Yes, I know.' I said. 'It's because of the rebels that were hiding in the mountains. No, that's not true. It's because I gave her a piece of steamed cake. The fragments of the sun's rays that had briefly dangled on her lashes at that moment, the colour of the sunset that crept into her eyes. That's it. As far as Gudnim is concerned, I believe that is the reason.'

'Are you all right? Are you sure you haven't gone queer under my influence? Let's go, anyway. Let me buy you a drink. Listen to me. As my statistics show, I don't know of a single case in which the spirit has descended on a male, so there's no chance of you becoming a male shaman – that's for sure, ha, ha.'

Could it be that I had come here with some fishing gear tucked away in my heart? Triggered off by the face of my wife as she turned over, and by the confirmation of the white strands in my hair, I wondered whether I had not set off with a length of angling line crammed in my inner pocket unaware of myself – a line like the spirit cord that raises the spirit of the dead.

The rain began to pour down again.

# THE GUEST

## Choi Hak

The wind? she thought, but no, it was not the wind. Someone was calling. The sound seemed to come from just outside the kitchen door one moment, then at the next from right down the valley.

'Is anyone in?'

The elderly woman who sat on the floor with her eyes on the television, half asleep, quickly smoothed her jacket. Resting one hand on the floor she turned down the volume. There was the sound of the door handle rattling. Obviously there was someone there. Who would have bothered to climb up this far? She heaved herself to her feet and opened the door. While she was gathering her rubber shoes and putting them on, she saw through the gap in the door a shadow bobbing. The tourists or mountain climbers who occasionally came this way would at the most take a peek at the main prayer-hall and then go. Nobody ever sought the residents of the monastery. The world being such a clever place, the telephone had reached as far as this monk's cell on the cliff top, so that if you had any business to discuss you could just dial the number from your own room. There was no need for you to waste your breath in climbing up this far.

'Who is it?' She tried to raise her voice as she walked across the kitchen but it did not come out as loudly as she had intended. She unfastened the clasp and opened the small door. It was a stranger, a man, perhaps forty. A delicate face with clear eyes. He had long hair like a youth and wore a bright red jersey, altogether a refreshing sight. He must have sweated quite a bit on his way up that steep hill. He held a thickish climbing jacket in his hand. He was of slightly less than average height and from his regular features and white skin it was obvious that he was a man of the city who rarely touched the soil with his fingers.

'Is the abbot not in?' As she saw him bow from the waist she, from habit, put her palms together in greeting.

'He has gone down to the main temple . . .' Her eyes automatically indicated the foot of the mountain. A sea of trees – oak, ash, and others. Through the thin branches of the oaks, the dappled roof ridge of the Great Hall could be seen. The asphalt road that wound through the valleys up to the main temple looked white in the distance like a length of thread, sparkling as it reflected the winter sun. In spring and autumn there was a constant flow of cars, large and small, but now, after a cold wind with dashes of snow had blown several times, there was no trace of them, and the road had become as deserted as the frozen path on which she fetched the water.

'Will he be back soon?' he asked as he sat on the edge of the narrow, wooden verandah.

'Yes, I am sure he will be here before the sun sets . . . where have you come from? If you are in a hurry you could give him a ring and ask him to come up . . .'

She felt uneasiness creeping on for no reason. Silly thing – you are too old for such feelings. She often reminded herself of this but she could not shake off a vague uneasiness when she was with people from the world outside, for the monk was the only person she knew in this temple, which was like an island in a distant sea. It's because I have been living at temples for so long, she thought. I can't help feeling strange with anyone from outside. And each time it happened she reproached herself. He said he was from Seoul. He had set out for this temple, he said, not because of any urgent business but just to stay for a few days in one of the guest rooms, and to take advantage of the fresh mountain air. Unlike most men of his age, he often smiled, showing white teeth. She liked his smiles. Just like a child. She thought he was not entirely unfamiliar. Then she started as she realized that what she was invoking before her eyes was her husband.

'I can't tell you yes or no without the Master,' she said. Leaving him alone in the sanctum, she went back to her own room behind the kitchen. She wondered whether she should go back to watching the television, but she turned it off altogether. About time to start cooking, she thought.

As she measured out the rice her hands stopped short, for she was wondering whether or not to put some more in for the stranger, but her hesitation was only momentary. She added some more.

Behind the backyard stood a straight rockface of unfathomable height that rose away above your head. On its way to the sky it thrust out in a bulge rather like somebody's forehead, so that you could not look straight up into the sky without stepping back and throwing your head back. For the first few days she had been there, she had feared that this rocky wall might fall in and at such thoughts she had felt a chill running through her whole body, but now perhaps because she was used to it, she no longer felt such fear. At the foot of it there was large hole as if part of the rock had been hollowed away. Inside this hollow was the well. It was not the sort where the water wells up from the bottom, but rather water that had seeped through cracks and collected there, clear and icy even in the summer. She now washed the rice with it, rubbing it hard against her palm. She rubbed so hard that she did not feel the numbing chill on her fingers. Silly man! Why couldn't he let me know, if he's fallen dead somewhere, at least the date, so that I could remember it and make sure he gets the sacrificial offerings. Damn it! Unaware of herself, these curses rose to her throat but she checked them in time as she wildly shook her head. 'Oh, no. I didn't mean that, Buddha of Mercy . . .' She purposely returned to the front via the stores and cast a quick glance in the direction of the sanctuary. The visitor was sitting on the verandah in the same manner as he had been a short while ago. His eyes were fixed on the ridge of the mountain beyond but he did not seem to take notice of anything in particular. What a strange man. To leave his comfortable home, wife and children to go to a poor place in the depths of the mountains and spend his own money to tremble with cold!

Meanwhile, the sun had gone down behind the hill but darkness had not yet filled the valley. Since the sun had gone down, the sound of the water flowing in the stream had grown clearer.

She put the rice in a cooking pot and lit a fire in the *ondol* stove for the extra bedroom beside the prayer hall, for she judged that it was too late for him to go back. Whatever the Master might say, she would first take the chill off the room where he would be sleeping, and then light the fire under the rice pot. She squatted down before the stove and lit the kindling twigs. When she saw they had all caught fire she stuffed more wood deep into the stove which ran under the floor. She straightened her back only when she saw that all the pieces were alight. Then with the end of her sleeve she brushed away the tears from the smoke. Do I still have tears left to wipe away? She would mumble to herself every time her eyes smarted from the fire as she fed the stove and they squeezed out.

'Can I help you?' Without her knowing the visitor had come up behind her. 'It will be all right, won't it, if I just keep putting the pieces on, one by one?' He came and sat beside her, giving her his usual quiet smile.

'It looks simple but you have to know how to do it.' Even as she said this she moved sideways a couple of steps to make room for him to sit down. With hands like a young girl's how can he make a fire, she thought, but on the other hand she could not help being curious to know how he would cope.

'It seems like ages since I last made a fire in a stove like this.' As he spoke he put several sticks into the fire. From the way he piled them on, taking care to leave gaps for the air, it was obviously not his first attempt. The flame was being sucked nicely into the flues under the floor. His face shone red as it reflected the fire. She liked his face aglow, as if he had had a glass of wine, better than the white face of earlier on.

'What do you do in Seoul, sir?' she asked as she handed him the poker.

'As you said, I am "sir" at a school.' As if he was preoccupied with the fire he answered without turning round.

'What kind of school?'

'A university.'

'A professor?'

'. . .'

'Why do you want to sleep at a temple when you have your own home? The food and the beds are rather poor here, you know.'

'But you have mountains, water and the sound of the wind.'

'Such common things. What's so good about them?'

'You have never lived in Seoul, have you, granny?'

'Well . . .'

'Seoul people regard a place like this as special. People here may think about Seoul like that, I suppose.'

'That's true – the way people accustomed to pure rice suddenly have cravings for barley mixed with it . . . but why have you come by yourself? You must have a wife and children.'

'They are a nuisance.'

'What a naughty man . . .' They both laughed. She no longer felt the uneasiness of earlier on, partly because she felt that somehow he was not entirely a stranger, even though she was sure it was their first meeting.

'How old are you granny?'

'Old enough for dying. Can't you see from my teeth? . . .'

'How old is that?'

'Sixty-three, coming up to sixty-four in the new year.'

'Not even seventy, so why do you call yourself old? You are still full of energy . . .'

'What's the point of going on and on? When you have no more strength and have to depend on others it's best to go quickly. I may look all right outwardly but inwardly I am rotten right through . . . it's all futile.'

'How long have you been at this place?'

'Not very long. About two months or so . . . it's because I love the Buddha that I move around from one monastery to another. Otherwise why would I want to be shut up deep in the mountains like this? To be honest, if it wasn't for the Buddha I would have dropped dead in the street a long time ago. He pulls me along and he says to me "Don't die yet". These days it is very difficult to find workers, that's why an old crone like me was taken on as a cook-member. You couldn't have dreamt of it in the old days.'

'It didn't have to be amidst such steep hills, did it? There are plenty of temples around.'

'But who would want me? It's only because this is such a remote place that they took me on . . . you can't imagine an exile more remote than this one, but now that I'm used to it I quite like it. There are only a few mouths to cook for, and not many visitors to bother you . . . ideal for an old thing like me. I am only sorry that I can't do better for the Master because I haven't much strength.'

'I can see how hard it must be to have to go up and down that hill, especially when it snows . . .'

'It's just one mile from the main temple but it's a whole day's walk for me. I take two steps and rest, another two and I have to halt . . . Look at this house – it's more like a swallow's nest hung on a cliff than a temple. Isn't it amazing that they could lay the foundations and raise the roof beam on the cliff-top like this?'

'I bet they had to take a lot of rests, like you, when they were building it.'

'A monk once told me that in the old days when they were planning to build it they offered prayers with such fervent dedication that it moved even the crows in the fields. It is said that these birds helped by carrying the tiles for the roof in their beaks. I quite believe it. Of course they would have done . . .'

'Is your husband dead?'

'My man?'

'Yes.'

'In the middle of talking about the goodness of the Buddha, why bring up the subject of that unlucky man . . .'

'Don't talk about him then if you don't want to.'

At a time like this, she noticed, he could smile playfully. The scent of the wood, she felt, was peculiarly sharp at the tip of her nose. Why doesn't the monk come back quickly.

'I don't even know whether he is dead or not, that silly old man, and by now I can't even remember his face. It has been such a long time.'

'Were you parted from him?'

'Of course I was. That's why I am on my own. Otherwise why would a woman with a husband leave home for a place like this?'

'Why did you part?'

'I don't know. Probably he didn't care for me . . . Oh, dear. It's not the time to be idle like this. I should be getting on with the cooking . . .' She got to her feet, her hand pressing her knee as she rose. As if to say she'd been talking nonsense, she wiped her lips and went across the yard.

Darkness was rising from the deeper end of the valley. The sound of the birds had become noticeably louder. She lit the fire of dry brush wood and twigs of oak in the stove over which the rice pot hung. Even while she watched the glowing flame the chill inside her heart did not easily give way. If he had come to experience temple life, why couldn't he just do it quietly and go away, instead of stirring up useless gossip? She thought it was because of him that these memories of her estranged husband had been revived. Hmm, she grunted as she wiped her nose with the end of her sleeve.

Her husband had been just like him, in the way that he was

not at all smart. Short of height, his hands had been soft and small like those of a girl. He had a white face with huge eyes as if he was faint-hearted . . . even the way he chatted in a gentle, low tone of voice was similar. With such effeminacy you wouldn't expect him to do really manly things, would you? Phew! Then there was something peculiar. On her lips he was always 'old man', 'old man', but the face floating before her eyes, even though faint, was always that of a young man. It did not seem possible for her even to imagine him as a man with a white beard and wrinkled face. When she recollected the gentle face of her husband at forty, she saw her own face close to his was, in the same way, different from the one she had now, topped with white hair. With her present face, she thought, she could not be side by side with that young husband. I quite understand, she thought, what people say about how a woman who loses her husband young ends up even in her hopeless old age living in the arms of a young man. A heartless man! Perhaps the draught was not working well. The fire kept blowing back.

It was twenty-one years since her husband had gone off to the USA, or was it England? For the first year or two he had sent regular letters from across the sea but then they had abruptly stopped. There had been no news of him, not so much as a rumour, so she didn't even know whether he was dead or alive. Barely three days passed without her writing to him at his original address without bringing back a single word of news. In no time, twenty years had gone. If there hadn't been an ocean lying between them, she would have set off looking for him even if she had to walk for ten years, for a hundred, but it was impossible. In this state she had lost her husband, and that was that.

'Wait for me, for sooner or later I will make a decision, either to come back myself or to bring you over here.' These had been his very words, but it had been a mistake to stay behind and trust in them. I should have followed him, even if I had to hide in his suitcase because I had no money for the fare. Or I should have kept him by holding on to the legs of his trousers, and insisting that we hold out in this country even if it meant his being sent to prison or beaten to death. A proper idiot that's what I am – I couldn't do any of these things so I let him go off by himself. It's all my fault.

Before their son Chori, then eight, had been run over by taxi on his way back from his grandfather's home, the three of them had lived happily together, envious of no one, even though they were not well off. Although the pay was poor, her husband was keen on his job as supervisor at a wig-making company. On her side, she earned some money by going from house to house doing casual work. As for Chori, he was a good intelligent boy of whom people were envious. Amidst the fun of bringing up a child and the pleasure of improving her home, ten years had passed in the blink of an eye, and when they were beginning to relax and enjoy life Chori, leaving his mum and dad behind, had so suddenly departed from this world. Her husband took to drinking, which he had not done before, and changed his job as often as he took his dinner. It was worse for her, she thought, in suffering a darkened life, but because of the changes occurring in her husband there was no room for her to weep and lament. It took two full years for her to settle him down afresh. She was only grateful that he had seen sense.

When he had sobered up, he gave up the life of a 'salary man' and set up a wig-manufacturing firm of his own. Perhaps their dead son Chori was helping them from the other side. Their business prospered from the first day. Even though without him they felt an emptiness in one corner, what an exciting and happy time that had been! Her husband never once failed to be energetic and smiling. For her, just to look at a face such as his filled her heart with happiness.

'Good things don't remain good for ever, and neither do bad things stay bad.' The words of the chief priest are quite right. Those happy times did not last ten years. With the export market being blocked, a chill atmosphere came sweeping across the factory. He could no longer cope with the business that he had set up. He was running about madly without sleep at night, but there was no way in which he could avoid his creditors. When his cheques bounced, the factory and his house were handed over to them. Overnight he became a criminal and had to flee. As for her, she had to move into a small rented room where she endured a life of waiting for him, not knowing when he would turn up.

After he had been in hiding for a year, he came home one winter evening under cover of darkness. Without even taking off his jacket, he said he was going to the United States. 'I am not just running away,' he said. 'I must make money. That is the only way I can survive, and you too. I don't want to end up by being known as a man who took other people's money. I must make money and pay it back. But it can't be done here. Even if I break my bones and burn my flesh it can't be done here. I will start all over again in America. Except for robbery I am prepared to do anything. As soon as I am settled I will invite you over. Within ten years I will return to this land, pay up all that I owe and then we'll live honourably.'

He left home there and then taking only a briefcase. 'I live on milk. Milk is my staple food and I am selling vegetables. I have obtained a driving licence, I have got a job as the driver of a tour bus . . .' She felt his strong will and determination to survive showing vividly in every word of every letter. 'Don't worry about me, I am all right. I am only concerned about you, I shall soon bring you over here . . .' Then the letters stopped. His determination to come back in ten years' time had not materialized even after twenty, let alone his promise to call her over. He was not the sort of husband who would easily abandon his promises nor was he one who would simply forget about her. Unless something dreadful had happened, it was impossible that the letters should have stopped.

The Master showed no sign of either approval or disapproval when she told him about the visitor, or after he had met the guest himself. He was always like that, so it was as good as saying that the visitor was allowed to stay there at least for this one night. He did not say 'Stay as long as you want,' but neither did he send him packing down the mountain. How kind of him, she thought to herself.

The three of them, the monk, the visitor and the old lady herself were having supper together at the same table. From time to time the monk spoke about his visit to the main house. From the way his eyes turned or the tone of his voice, it was plainly directed at her. As she cautiously responded she was inwardly anxious, lest his manners made the visitor feel unwelcome. Her only comfort was that the man from Seoul was eating this rough temple food with relish.

'What do you specialize in?' the monk asked, as if in passing, while picking up some dressed leaves of perilla with his chopsticks. The woman started at such an unexpected question. She did not understand what he meant until she realized it was directed to the man from Seoul. Then she was belatedly pleased. It was the first question to be directly addressed to him.

'I am in electrical engineering, sir,' he said as he picked up a piece of mooli pickle. She was pleased at the way he replied with natural composure.

'There is no hope of people like us ever understanding such things however much you tried to explain it to us.' He gave a low laugh and the guest smiled after him as if in agreement.

'Judging from your accent you were not born in Seoul?'

'No, Pusan is my home town.'

'I thought so. I am from there too. Were you educated there?'

'You could say that – I went as far as high school there.'

'. . .'

The visitor seemed to interpret the silence that followed as a question about his college. Momentarily his eyes hovered between the woman and the monk. 'It so happened that from then on I studied in America.'

America! The old woman nearly let go of her spoon. Once again the face of her husband floated before her eyes. Unaware of herself, she was blankly staring at the guest's face when the monk aroused her. 'Don't go day-dreaming again – just eat up your supper,' he said, and turned to the guest.

'Please excuse her. She goes like this every time the word "America" crops up. A long time ago her husband went there and she has been out of touch with him ever since – so she says.' The way he ended the sentence was a little strange. Did he mean to suggest that even though she said so, it could have been the product of a lonely old woman's imagination? A soundless smile that momentarily rose to his lips was queer too.

'What have I done now . . .' she said as she nervously pulled the soup bowl nearer.

'I see . . .' The visitor did not look at either of them. Mooli pickle, perilla leaves, and then soya-beans and the sprouts . . . he seemed to concentrate solely on using his chopsticks to pick them up from the side dishes one after another as if following some prearranged plan. The monk said with a look of embarrassment, 'Madam, you might as well put it out of your mind completely. Do you think it's possible that you would never have heard a thing about him? It has been over twenty years . . .'

'I don't think about anything.'

'You say so, but you really can't give up, can you? As soon as you hear someone has been to America, you prick up your ears, don't you?' She was silent. A monk who has never been married and never had a wife or a child – how could he ever understand this heart of mine. She chewed the grains of rice with hard deliberation.

'Our guest who has been over there would know best. How big is America? Ten times, twenty times the size of our country, would you say? And the number of people as well – how can you expect any one to meet any one else . . . it would be difficult indeed.' The topic of America brought an unusual liveliness into the tone of his voice.

'Yes.'

He will pick up some bean sprouts next, she thought.

'How long were you over there?' He seemed to be disappointed with the rather brief reply. He means to annoy me even more. She thought him hateful. As she had expected the man from Seoul picked up some sprouts.

'I was over there a long time. When I finished my studies I got a job and stayed on. I have been back home just over four years now.'

'You spent all your youthful years in America, it seems?'

'You could say that.'

'Where were you living mainly?' She put in as she plucked up her courage. The visitor still did not look up at her.

'Well. While I was at college I was mainly in Texas and Los Angeles, but when I got a job it was at a place called Seattle.'

'L.A.? Is it right that there are many of our people living there?'

Hwang Tai-yon. She knew she should have asked whether he had known a man called Hwang Tai-yon but she could not bring herself to say it. If only the monk was not there, she would certainly have asked. Sixty-four years of age. Short of height, slightly fat lips, long ears hanging down his cheeks, double-lidded eyes, a square forehead . . . and what else? Anyway, have you never even heard of the name, Hwang Tai-yon?

'Yes. There are many of them.' His reply was too simple.

'Over twenty thousand, I hear?' The Master intervened again.

'Yes, the officially known figures are twenty thousand or twenty-five but if you add up all those not officially registered, the rumour goes that there'd be over fifty thousand.'

What does the number matter? If you are fated to meet someone, then you do. Hwang Tai-yon, have you ever met him? That is what I should like to know. She was completely losing her appetite. How hateful the monk was.

'I thought so. I heard about it from a monk who has been over there. It is wonderful, he says. Millers, pawnshops . . . there's everything we have here, even fortune-tellers – isn't that so? Even if you can't speak a word of English you can get by with no inconvenience?'

'That's true.'

'If you had been living over there for so long it must have been hard to come back. It must have needed courage.'

'That's true, but however long you live there it is still someone else's country, isn't it? It can never be as good as your own. I was thinking like that all the time . . . fortunately for me I knew someone who wanted to have me back, so I came.'

'That was very wise of you. All the good things you've learned should be made use of in our own country. You can't waste it on someone else's, can you?' He sounded just like a member of Parliament. After supper the monk and the guest went into their respective rooms, and she was left with the washing-up. As she polished the brass bowls, squatting on a piece of wooden plank, she mumbled the strange name of the city in America, L.A., L.A. Her husband had told her that he was driving a bus there. Didn't he say that while other people worked until five he volunteered to work until ten and even till midnight as long as there was the demand. He had said his income was quite good. It must be within that city that he was living if he was still alive, or buried if he was dead. It was not the first time that she had met someone who had been there, but she had never been as flustered as she was now. Was it because the guest resembled him? Or was it because he had sought this deep mountain of his own accord? Anyway, there was something strange about it. The magpies, the harbingers of a good omen, had been calling particularly hard from the morning.

The sound of the big bell at the main house came up from the valley. The deep heavy sound shook the woods and the darkness. It was time for evening prayers. The Master of the small temple threw on his vestments as the bell sounded, and went into the prayer hall. It was only a small room with one lone image of the Buddha of Medicine. Soon there came the sound of the scripture being chanted and the beating of the wooden gong. She loved the voice of the Master reciting. Whenever she heard it, it seemed infinitely powerful and rang clear. It was quite different from the voices of the monks at Heyam Temple and Daisung-am where she had been previously. It fluctuated beautifully and held smoothly to the punctuations . . . When she heard it even in the kitchen, she felt her heart being sanctified of its own accord. She felt happy to be a temple cook.

When she had quickly done the washing-up, she went to the room next to the hall. She meant to put another batch of firewood in the stove. What she had put on before supper would have taken the chill off the floor but was hardly enough to keep his back warm through the night. She was deliberately noisy as she stuffed in the wood but he did not bother to look out. Listening carefully, she suspected there was no one there.

'Are you warm enough?' She shouted in front of the sliding door. There was no reply. She opened it and found the room empty. Only a jumper hung on the hook on the wall. At first she thought he must be taking part in the prayers. Then she realized that the time of the service was over. Unless he had gone over to the monk's room she could not think of anywhere else he was likely to be. After hanging around the monk's room she gave up and went back to her own place by the kitchen. Her heart smarted but she nursed it saying there was still time tomorrow. What could he have to talk about with the Master for so long? . . . She stared at the television without hearing what the people on it were saying. There had been a time when she thought perhaps it was because he had a child somewhere that he did not come back to her. When she thought about how upset he had been after losing their boy, Chori, it seemed quite plausible. What was the good of a wife who was no longer fertile? Where you don't have to worry about what people say or hear about you why not marry again? He may have done that, that silly idiot of a man . . .

As he took the cup of tea that the Master handed over to him, Suh Sukho's lips twitched several times as if by habit. The scent of the tea reached his nostrils.

'. . . It was probably in seventy-two or -three that I first made his acquaintance. It was not long after I moved to L.A. from Texas. I was hard at work earning my fees for college. I was employed at a car-wash where he often used to come. Apart from a vague friendliness among fellow exiles, he was particularly kind to me. He was like an elder brother. He seemed to have established some sort of foundation. He said he was going to buy a minibus and set up a business of his own. I found out much later that he was ill even at this stage although he did not tell me. He was suffering from diabetes. Some time after that he really did buy two buses and set up a company. A company in name only, with no office or staff. His apartment was his office, and he, the managing director was also the driver. He mainly carted round tourists from Korea, and I worked with him for about six months, sometimes as the driver and at other times as an assistant. I learned a lot from him as to the ways of getting by in the world. He was an amazing character. The business was doing quite well then, but I never saw him buy himself a meal, or even a cup of coffee. He seemed to have stopped communicating with his wife at some time before that. It was purely because of his illness. After I moved to Seattle I didn't see him for a long time, probably four or five years . . . but I heard from someone that overnight he had lost the company that had been prospering. Apparently he had been deceived by a fellow Korean. To become naturalized, he underwent a mock marriage with an American, and that was the cause of his decline. It is a common occurrence. I felt terribly sorry for him but never managed to go and see him. After that we lost touch. I think it was in July of eighty-two, during the summer holidays, I went back to L.A., and with some friends from college with whom I used to be involved in Mission work I went to visit a mental hospital run by the State. Quite unexpectedly I saw him there. He had changed so much that I did not recognize him but he did me.

'The miserable state he was in is beyond description. I could see that he would not live much longer. On top of the diabetes he was an alcoholic . . . As he grabbed hold of my hand he wept endlessly, tears flowing. Then he started talking about his wife. When you go back please make sure you see her for me, he said. He said there had not been a day or a moment when he did not think of that poor woman. He handed me two thousand dollars that he had managed to save, with great hardship, and asked me to use it for her benefit. He pleaded with me not to tell her that I had met him. He could not bear to hurt her afresh by bringing up the man whom she would have forgotten after bitter grieving. The anniversary of his death is on 21 September. No one was at his bedside when it happened. I would be very much obliged, sir, if you would set up a tablet for him behind the altar and comfort his lonely spirit with your prayers. I will leave without telling her anything.

'Ever since I came back I have been trying hard to find out where she was but it wasn't easy. There was no trace of her in her place of origin . . . The only clue I had was that she originally came from Kwangsok in Nonsan, so you can imagine how hopeless it was. Every time the vacation came round I set my students from that area the task of finding her and it was thanks to them that I was able to come here. Please allow me, sir, to leave this money with you – this is the original amount that he gave me along with the interest. Whether you give it to her now or keep it for her for a future emergency is up to you. In the same way as my friend trusted me with this I leave it now with you. When I saw her yesterday how fast my heart was beating. You must tell her. Tell her everything as you saw and heard and felt about it, I kept urging myself, but I could not open my mouth in the end. It was not only because of what he had said . . . I don't know why. You are the nearest person to her now, so, please allow me to unburden myself and hand it over to you.'

As soon as breakfast was over the man who had said he would stay for a few days was saying he was going down. What a silly man!

'I made a phone call to Seoul. There's some urgent business and they want me to go back at once.' He was even making excuses which was quite unnecessary. If you want to go, go then. I am used to people treating the temple in that way, she said inwardly, but could not help feeling a little sorry.

The cloudy sky was very low as if it was going to bring down a flurry of snow. To see him off, the Master was walking with him as far as the corner of the pagoda. He had never done that before.

'I have enjoyed my stay. Thank you very much and goodbye.' The monk and guest bowed to each other at the same time.

'Granny, please take care of yourself and live long.' She had expected he would go away without taking any notice of her, but he was also taking leave of her.

'Goodbye.' What she should have said was 'Do you know Hwang Tai-yon?' but what came out of her lips was different. After watching him from behind as he walked down the stone steps, she also took a step down the flight unaware of herself, but, no, the Master firmly held her arm.

# SHE KNOWS, I KNOW AND GOD KNOWS BUT . . .

Park Wan-suh

'BY the way, where's the bereaved woman gone to? Has she passed out from grief or something?'

'Passed out? – not likely. From what I hear she is uncommonly shrewd. No doubt she's busy planning her own future.'

'Disgusting! She could at least have waited until after the third sacrifice. That wouldn't be too late, would it? She's not in any danger of being turned out.'

'You're right. If only she'd show a bit more dignity, like the lady of the house, at least until the funeral tomorrow is over, let alone the third sacrifice. It would be saving their face.'

'You only expect decent behaviour from somebody with standards. From the beginning, I knew that she couldn't be expected to show much decorum. Jintai's mum's not as clever as she looks. Or she's been taken in. I can't understand what made her bring in such an old beggar.'

'From what I've heard, she wasn't exactly a beggar. She used to go round the market in Songnam selling things out of a basket . . .'

'No, it wasn't Songnam. Didn't she used to sell vegetables under the railway bridge in Jamsil?'

'Jamsil's right, but not under the railway bridge. I think it was in Saemaul market, that she first came to the notice of Jintai's mum. She used to go round selling things like elastic and socks from a bundle.'

'Wherever it was, I'm the one who knows what she was really like when she came here – literally a beggar. Shaggy hair and a short-sleeved jacket soaked in dirt and sweat. It stank. And the dirt in her nails, between her toes and on her cracked heels –

if you collected it all up, it would've been enough to make a briquette.'

'You're a liar!' The women burst into laughter. They were friends of Jintai's mum, the eldest daughter-in-law of the dead man and frequent visitors. Some from her schooldays, others from her credit union, flower-arrangement society or neighbours. As soon as the old man had drawn his last the day before, they had called to offer help. They talked a lot and laughed a lot too. Yesterday at least they had been mindful not to speak or laugh too loudly but today they seemed to have forgotten.

'Should we be laughing so loudly?'

'It's all right. After all it's a happy release.'

'If only she had held out a little bit longer – I mean Jintai's mum.'

'What do you mean?'

'I mean it's not even three years since she dragged in that old woman. If only she had gone on looking after her father-in-law herself, how much simpler it would have been. It would be a real happy release.'

'It's easy to say that three years is a short time, but it's not so easy to wait on a widowed father-in-law who's had a stroke, is it? Besides, as the saying goes "However faithful a son and a daughter-in-law may be, they are not as good as a bad wife." It was real filial care on her part to provide him with a woman.'

'She really is a rare example of a virtuous daughter-in-law. How sadly she cried yesterday. She took to her bed and hasn't touched a grain of food! What's the good of having real daughters? They were all pretending to be surpressing their tears, with tightly pressed lips. You could tell by their dry beady eyes. The daughters are no use, nor the son. The only gem is this daughter-in-law who has waited on him right up to the day he died.'

'That reminds me, we had better take her some warm milk or something. Being a virtuous daughter is all very well but she's thoroughly worn out. What can you expect when she is refusing to eat anything?'

'Yes, we'd better. Let's take her some soup and milk, and see how she is. I've never yet heard of a daughter-in-law dying after her father-in-law. What a darling idiot.'

When the women had all scuttled away to the inner quarters where Jintai's mother lay stretched out in bed, the kitchen was empty.

Songnam-*dek*, crouching out of sight in the tiny back room attached to the kitchen, now opened the door a crack and peered through. 'Bloody women – they would have to go about in a gang.' She mumbled to herself as she clucked her tongue. They did not seem to know how to divide up the work or realize what there was to be done. All they did was huddle together yakking away, busier with their mouths than their hands. When they took off all together, the kitchen was really in a mess. On the gas range all four rings were on, the blue flames flaring. Something was vigorously boiling, and the floor was strewn with half-trimmed bunches of spring onions, half-scraped pieces of mooli and a slipper flung upside-down. Blocking the door was a large party table so untidy it was impossible to tell whether it was in the process of being laid out or being cleared away.

When she thought about the insults she had suffered the day before, she thought she ought never again to take any notice of them, but she stealthily crept out to turn down the ring on which the soup was boiling over and after making sure the pork was cooked by sticking a chopstick into it, she turned it off. The pollack stew seemed to be simmering just right. She tasted it. It could do with a little more salt, but not bad. Alas, it was a dreadful mistake to whet her appetite. All of a sudden a fierce desire to eat surged up in her. Her intestines writhed like a dragon screaming in its death throes. Since the previous dawn, when the old man had passed away, she had eaten almost nothing. While his daughter-in-law grieved without taking anything, it did not seem right for her, as his wife, though only in name, to tuck in. Into the room where Jintai's mum lay stretched out with grief everything you could think of was taken – milk, pine-nut soup, yoghurt, *baccus* and ginseng tea, but no one paid any attention to her. Not only was she forbidden to come into the kitchen, but no one invited her to the meal table or took anything to her room.

The kitchen was full of food. Even the leftovers on the plates to be washed up – slices of pork, fried fillet of fish, vegetables, dregs of stew, and rice in soup – would have made a sumptuous meal for an empty stomach. At the thought that those pretentiously hygienic women would put it all into the bin without hesitation, she felt a tightness of the heart. Why not quickly pick up a piece of pork, wrap it in a piece of *kimchi*, and put it down her throat? She was about to do it but drew back her hand in a reflex reaction as the word 'dignity' rose to her mind. During the three years since she had undertaken to look after the old man, the phrase she had heard most often from Jintai's mother was 'Please remember the dignity of our family.'

Songnam-*dek* had some bad habits. For example, she felt comfortable only when she wore a calf-length skirt fastened tightly round her waist with a cloth-belt; except in the worst of winter she could not bear to wear socks, for they stifled her; she was a voracious eater for whom rice tasted as sweet as honey and she could eat any amount of it with stewed radish leaves or sour *kimchi*; her voice was too loud, as if she had a large bell on her throat; her buttocks wobbled from side to side when she walked, a habit acquired from her days as a trader carrying heavy weights on the top of her head; whenever she heard the calls of the traders as they passed through the alley, some pushing their wares in carts and others carrying them in baskets, she would hurry out with big strides and loved to haggle over the price of things she was not going to buy; she used great swear words at the end of every phrase, and if she didn't, she felt queasy as if she had eaten the rice without side dishes. For a woman such as her to be trained and polished into such average gentility as she now possessed was partly the result of constant and chilly reminders from Jintai's mother, but even more due to her own perseverance, as if enduring a terrible torture. When her endurance wavered she had gritted her teeth and reminded herself of the flat of thirteen *pyong*. When she thought that this flat, which her son, a casual labourer due to a lack of education, could hardly have afforded even with the wages of a lifetime, could be obtained by only a few years' endurance, her buttocks unconsciously waggled with joy even while in bed. That she had a married son, a daughter-in-law and a grandchild, was a well-kept secret. Not knowing that one day her fate would turn out this way, she had given it out that she was an unfortunate old woman living on her own, as for an old woman to work so hard when she had a son would bring shame on him. Luckily for her, Jintai's mother, while making a great fuss about her manners lest they disgraced the family, never asked her about her past. She seemed to have an instinctive aversion to the past of such a vulgar woman. It showed vividly in her words as she extended her pleas to respect the honour of the family.

'Songnam-*dek* granny, can't you ever stop showing the marks of the time when you used to be chased away from one place to another with a basket on your head? Aren't you ashamed of yourself? For heaven's sake, try to understand that I've never told anyone that you come from that kind of background. I've hidden it even from the children and their father, and whenever you betray it, with no warning, I feel faint with dread. If you could only hide it, don't you see, you could pass as a lady in the inner quarters of a genteel family?'

She had heard such words till her eardrums hardened. But the friends of Jintai's mother knew and had gossiped about her past though only in the manner of nit-picking, in whispers or with lowered voices. Today they were doing it with no inhibitions, speaking loudly as if they wanted her to hear. Was it that the genteel and demure mistress of the house had herself spread the story as soon as the old man had drawn his last breath? Or had she told them all from the beginning, while playing a wicked trick on her? With her dull and simple mentality, Songnam-*dek* could not understand it. In fact, she did not mind her origins being revealed nor was she ashamed of them. It was true that her life had been harsh, and she had more often been chased away with her basket on her head, than allowed to sit in one place and sell her wares. But she firmly believed that it was not her own fault. At the judgement in the next world, she believed, it would be the market stewards with their habit of harassing the street traders who would be punished, and not the likes of her, the traders who had been chased around. So she was not shy about the things that her mistress tried to hush up.

'Let them chatter and babble to their heart's content. No one's without dust when they are shaken, as the saying goes. I have nothing to be afraid of.' With this mental stance she was not inclined to blame the women for making fun of her poor origins. If my peddling in Moran Market under the railway bridge or in the Saemaul market is such a novelty, how about the way I used to carry ten bundles of garlic on my head, with a hundred heads in each, and never a wobble. If they knew about this, those bloody women, they'd stretch out stiff with surprise, beside Jintai's mother. She even felt a sense of amusement rising in her mind.

That she could feel so tolerant was probably due to certain misgivings that she began to harbour about Jintai's mother. There was, to begin with, the wicked way in which she had spread the story of her origins, after making such a show of kindness in hiding it, which Songnam-*dek* hadn't even asked her to do. That was something she would never understand. On top of this, even more hateful, was Jintai's mother's attitude to herself which had suddenly changed so drastically.

At dawn yesterday, when the old man had died, her show of grief as his daughter-in-law was such that it caused a commotion. Everyone – her husband, the chief mourner, Jintai and even the girl, Jinsuk – were so involved in comforting her that they took little notice of the dead man. It was Songnam-*dek* who, after making sure that his breathing had really stopped, straightened his limbs, laid his hands on his stomach, gathered his feet together, straightened his neck, and finally covered his body with a sheet. She did it all devotedly, with great care. Then she brought out a jacket that he used to wear from the chest to be used when inviting the spirit. That was, to her knowledge, the correct procedure for a funeral. She did not know much beyond that, it is true, but, more than that, she had the sense to know that it was not her business to interfere but to leave it to Jintai's mother to carry on from there when she came out of the keening. After being entirely tied up with waiting on this man, the sudden release made her feel rather empty and forlorn, and belatedly she felt tears rising in her eyes. As she quietly sobbed she wondered what she should do next and decided to cook 'The Rice for the Messenger', a meal for the Messenger from the other world who would come to receive the soul of the dead. She had finished washing the rice, had put it on the cooker and was just about to strike a match when Jintai's mum, having stopped wailing, ran up. Unlike a grieving woman, she was bursting with energetic hatred. 'My goodness, what do you think you are doing?'

'I am going to cook the rice for the Messenger . . . by the way, you had better let people know about it as fast as you can, and don't worry about the kitchen. Am I right in thinking that the inviter of the spirit ought to be someone who hasn't yet seen the body? I expect, these days, the undertakers will do that as well.'

'Songnam-*dek*, can't you go in at once and keep out of sight? Where do you think you are? How dare you tell me to do this and that?' She glared at her as she said these ferocious words. Songnam-*dek* felt as if she had been struck a blow on the head. She was numb and could not find a word to say. When the old man had been alive, she had at least been regularly addressed as 'Songnam-*dek* granny'. This was the name, meaning 'Old Lady from Songnam', commonly used not only by the family, but also by Jintai's aunts, the daily helpers and visitors who frequented the house. To tell the truth, she had not from the beginning been pleased with this name for it seemed to betray their agreement.

When she had first been invited into the family by Jintai's mother it had not been merely as a servant to wait on her father-in-law, but as a new mother-in-law. She had repeatedly been promised that she would be courteously treated as mother-in-law and when her husband's father died she would be given the thirteen *pyong* flat that still legally belonged to him. She had been happy enough when she lived alone with him in that flat. After a stroke, he was paralysed on one side of his body, but he could walk quite well with some support from her. He had a good appetite and he was generous. At first, she had been slightly put off by his nagging her to economize, but soon she came to realize that he only wanted to save a little from the tight allowance given to him by his daughter-in-law so that he would have something to give to her. They had lived like that for just over two years when he had a second stroke. He became bedridden, with his mind drifting, and had to use a bedpan. When things came to this, Jintai's mother, proclaiming it was her filial duty, insisted on his joining the family. So Songnam-*dek*, leaving the life at the small flat into which she had put so much affection and devotion, followed the old man into his son's home.

She didn't remember exactly being addressed as 'Mother' by Jintai's mum even when they had lived apart. Once the two families were joined, she was commonly called 'Songnam-*dek* granny' and felt a bit put out at first, but she soon got used to it. There were times when she wished they would drop the '*dek*' bit which specifically indicated that she was a woman from outside the family. If only they would call her 'Songnam granny', that would sound more amicable. But she had never even mentioned the subject. That was about the limit of her desires. From her side, equally, she had never contemplated regarding a woman like Jintai's mother with her overflowing aristocratic airs, as her daughter-in-law. Probably because her feelings were like that anyway, her anger and revulsion at receiving such contemptuous treatment as being called 'Songnam-*dek*', with the granny bit dropped, did not last long. All she did was to feel sorry for her hasty temperament, thinking to herself, what a pity that she is so impatient when there is no real hurry. She could have waited until the funeral was over and the reckoning cleared up and then they could have parted as unrelated people. What she meant by the 'reckoning' was of course handing over of the thirteen-*pyong* flat.

At the sound of the friends of Jintai's mother all rushing back to the kitchen she quickly retreated into her room. The only edible thing she held in her hand was the tail of a mooli radish. Peeling the outer skin, she started to crunch it. Being the tail end, it tasted rather strong and gave her an acid stomach.

'Of all sorrows, the sorrow of hunger is the worst . . .' At the thought of the old man she could not finish it. 'When my own husband with whom I slept and who fathered my child died, I was still so young and the thought of a life ahead with the task of feeding myself and the kid was so enormous, like a great mountain, that I had no room to shed a tear or even a drop from my nose. They said I was heartless, and look at me now,' she thought. 'It is because I am not as desperate as I was then, but if my husband saw me like this he'd be jealous.' She pressed her eyes with the hem of her skirt.

When she had lived in the flat with the old man, just the two of them, she had taken great care of him, preparing tasty bits of this and that for each meal time. He had a good appetite by nature, to which was added the greed of an elderly person with nothing much to do, so he had enjoyed his food. Now and again he would complain that they were spending too much on it. He did not seem to know that his daughter-in-law had promised her that she would inherit the apartment. She knew that what he meant was to save a few pennies from the monthly allowance his daughter-in-law gave him and give it to her, so she did not mind his nagging. After he had the second stroke and moved into his son's house, his appetite did not diminish but Jintai's mother would not give him more than half a bowl of rice, or a half-packet when it was noodle. When it was lunch-time she came into the kitchen, cut in half a packet of noodles, put one half away in the drawer and left the other saying, 'There you are. Get it ready for my father.' When she said this, how heartlessly smart her voice sounded. The old man, unable now even to speak, showed his desire for more food with his eyes. When she recollected those eyes filled with sadness, as after noisily sucking in the curly strands of noodles he lay on his side, looking in turn at the bowl nearly empty and her face, she was even now afraid of Heaven. In the future, she thought, she would never sleep properly on a night when the lightning struck. What else could I do? Whether aimed at heaven or herself, she was making clumsy excuses. It was true, there was absolutely nothing she could have done about it. Jintai's mother never allowed her in to the kitchen except to boil the half packet of noodles and kept even the refrigerator locked up. Songnam-*dek* herself could eat her fill but her meals were taken in the dining-room with the daily helper and she dared not save anything to take round to him.

'It is for your own good I am doing this, Songnam-*dek*,' Jintai's mother would say when she pleaded with her to increase the amount of his food just a little, pretending she cared about her. 'All he does is to put food in at one end and bring it out at the other. Give him as much as he wants and how would you cope with all that excrement? And what about the washing?' Indeed, the old man, despite his small intake put out an enormous quantity. It would hardly be an exaggeration to say that she had lived day and night buried in excrement and urine. He soiled the nappies, trousers and the bed-sheets faster than she could replace them and he whimpered. What a good job there was a drier. She could not think how she would have coped without it. Several times a day she thanked that wonderful machine. In proportion to his taking in little and bringing out much, the old man grew more emaciated day by day. Once of good bearing, he was now reduced to showing a bony ribcage, his knee-bones sticking out like the gnarls of a tree while his thighs shrivelled. Even now she was inclined to believe that he did not so much die as waste away.

While he had still been alive it was Jintai's mother who restricted her from going in and out of the kitchen. Now he was dead, it was the husband who turned her out of the dead man's room. As they laid him out in the room in which he passed away, she thought it was her duty to be there. Then Jintai's father in a very crude manner told her to go and stay somewhere out of sight as it was not seemly for the visitors coming to present their condolences.

'What do you mean by "not seemly"?' If it had only been his mother, she would have asked this and reasoned with her, but she was too timid before his father so she just obeyed him and went out. Day after day she had cleaned up the mess and washed him, turning his body this way and that, but now she was forbidden even to watch either the shrouding or the placing of the body in a coffin. After it was put in the coffin, she had a chance to catch a glimpse of it over the shoulders of others. It was lacquered so shiny that you could see your face reflected in it, and it even had a patterned inlay of mother-of-pearl and it was an enormous size. The luxurious appearance and the size of the coffin reinforced her feelings that he had not died but wasted away. He had been progressively shrinking in size and weight until the day his life was extinguished, she thought, so the coffin must be indeed as good as empty.

When they came back to the kitchen, the women, with one accord, began to praise the filial piety of Jintai's mother who had exhausted herself in grieving over the death of her father-in-law, and at the same time to blame her as well. And then somehow their talk went in rather a strange direction. 'I say, did you ever think about this?' The speaker started to giggle.

'What?'

'When the thought comes to me I start to laugh even when I'm in bed.'

'Come on, out with it! You're not dumb! Can't you do anything better than laugh?'

'Don't you wonder whether the second wife – Songnam-*dek* and the late master of this house ever slept together?'

'Slept together? I see, you minx. What a thought . . .'

'I sometimes wondered about that too. When they used to live in the flat he looked so well. He had a well-built body and his mind was clear . . . he could have done it every night.'

'Well-built indeed! He'd already had a stroke and on one side his limbs were quite useless, don't you remember?'

'That doesn't have to mean the middle one was useless too, does it? Unless you have seen it yourself.'

'Awful bitch! Whenever you're around you make me swear. I shouldn't have anything more to do with a woman like you.'

'Don't then. However much you pretend to be genteel, your husband has got hold of another woman at this moment upstairs.'

'How did you find that out?'

'While I was taking the food round.'

'Well, any man who didn't seize the chance while he was at a funeral – I'd call him an idiot. What's your husband up to? Is he campaigning for the election?'

'No, he's busy gambling. With his mouth shut tight and eyes burning bright like a lamp.'

'I wish him luck. He may earn something big towards his election funds.'

'These two! Whenever they are together they seem to get at each other. Stop it now and let's get back to the main discussion.'

'What was the main discussion?'

'Whether they slept together or not.'

'You mean whether it was possible or not?'

'If it hadn't been, do you think she would have stayed on?'

'How old do you think she is? She's too old to remarry for that anyway, isn't she?'

'I don't know how old she is but she's vigorous and rough.'

'Being vigorous is one thing, but what has being rough got to do with it?'

'Of course it has. Being rough means not refined, but simple and if you are simple you don't have much interest in anything else.'

'I suppose that makes sense. With my husband, you know, he gave up his job belatedly, went on to get a MA and then doctorate. After that he got a job as a college lecturer. Since then, he's hopeless, not only has his hair gone white, but he can't do it any more. It's the same with me I suppose. Since I started doing various work as a volunteer and being mentally active, I seem to have lost interest in that sort of thing.'

'Listen to her! Whoever it is, it's a matter of how old you are. We have reached a certain age, that's all. It's not that you are particularly noble.'

'So you are telling us that we have reached the age of decline?'

'That's right. Are you sorry for yourself? Anyway we live in a time when people mature early and grow old early – don't you think so?'

'What a pompous thing to say! Even bringing in the age we live in! When you admit that you are growing prematurely old yourself, what a nasty thing to speculate on the relationship between two people who have both lived to a good age.'

'I've good reason for it. Obviously you haven't heard that strange tale from Jintai's mother.'

'What tale?'

'Well . . .' The woman started to laugh as she dragged to the end of the sentence. It was sensuous laughter appropriate to induce lewd imaginations.

'Don't be a tease. Come out with it.'

'She told me this. The old woman is pretty smart. Since she took charge of cleaning up the mess she became quite bossy, probably thinking that there was no one else who could do it but herself. Once he had relieved himself she would call for several basins of water to be brought along to the room. It's all very well to keep him clean but, sometimes, she seemed to take too long over it, so Jintai's mother peeped in now and again and what do you think she saw? She was fingering and fumbling endlessly with that part of his body.'

'My goodness, how awful!'

'Oh, it's weird.' The women broke into cackles, some screaming like teenage girls.

Just listen to those silly women! If they had looked after any children of their own they would know how fiddly it is to have to wipe the bottom of a boy after he has had a shit. How can they imagine such awful things about old people? Songnam-*dek* shook with anger and her teeth chattered. It had been a really dreadful job to clean up the excrement all pressed on and messed up. Especially wiping the leathery and wrinkled male organ demanded unusually steady nerves and patience. It happens so often, so why not make a quick job of it? – such thoughts had crossed her mind but she reminded herself that if she was negligent about this job, and still intended to have the flat, that would be dishonest and it would be a thief's mind and I'd deserve to be punished. So she had taken meticulous care while swallowing hard the rising nausea as if enduring a severe torture.

She was disgusted not so much by the prattling of the women as the revulsion she felt towards Jintai's mother who had spread such nasty stories. The whole of her guts trembled making her shake from top to bottom like a dog that has had a basin of washing-up water thrown over it.

Someone said, 'I knew she would be like that.'

'Like what?'

'Can't you see it from the way she walks? Wobbling her buttocks from side to side like this.' She must have been actually demonstrating it for a cackle of laughter rose with gasps of breath. For the old lady, still trembling, this was throwing a handful of burning coals over her. Her face mercilessly burned.

'I couldn't even imitate it.'

'No, not with your sort of buttocks.'

'You see her walking, so you can guess, can't you? That sort of gait indicates vigour in that way.'

Apart from the lure of the flat that was being offered, what had initially persuaded her to take on serving the old man had been the fact that at first glance he had showed no sign of sexuality. However much she wanted the flat she would not have liked to be forced into a sexual relationship at her age. She had been widowed at the height of womanhood but as the worries of feeding the family loomed before her like a great mountain she had rarely thought about men, and by now she had developed a fastidious dislike of sex. If the old man had belied her guess at the first meeting, she would have shaken him off and run away as if from a fire, despite the flat or even a whole house. Thankfully, he had treated her like a trustworthy friend, and she had not the slightest fear at the prospect of meeting her husband in the after world. He would understand regardless of what anyone might say that all through her life she had lived for only one husband.

'All in all, I feel sorry for the old madam.'

'Well, she must have had some good times in the beginning.'

'Don't be silly. With her vigorous buttocks and that old man after a stroke – what good would that be to her?'

'When you think about it, I'm sorry for the old man too.'

'Having a too powerful woman could have shortened his life, couldn't it? He might have hung on for a few more years.'

'He's had a good life and a spate of passion at the end of it. There's nothing to feel sorry about. It's about time Jintai's mum had a chance to enjoy life. People like you who don't have their in-laws in the same house with them will never know, will they?'

'That's true. You're quite right. But what happens if the old woman decides to stay on and claim her rights as mother-in-law? Do you think she would?'

'I don't think so. You can tell from the way she behaves – as soon as he passed out she withdrew and hasn't shown up anywhere in his room or the kitchen, as if to say it has nothing to do with her.'

'Do you think she's been registered as a member of the family?'

'Who? Songnam-*dek*? Don't be daft. Do you think a clever woman like Jintai's mum would do such a thing and cause trouble for later days?'

'So, give her some money and send her away – that will be it then.'

'About the money, I understand she has been smarter than Jintai's mum. The fact of the matter was that the two of them living in that small apartment had the same amount of housekeeping money as this big family here, Jintai's. Even so, by the end of the month they were whining as if they didn't have a penny left. Jintai's mother couldn't believe it so she occasionally popped in to see how they were getting on and she was shocked to see how poorly they ate. Where do you think all that money went? After living like that for over two years, she must have accumulated a small fortune. But having a wife must have been something very special for him even at that age so that he wanted to give her more money despite being fed so poorly. He went behind her back and asked his daughter-in-law for more. Every time it happened she was very upset – I remember her telling me this several times.'

'But as a man who had been fairly well off in his day didn't he have any other source of income except the son and his wife?'

'I expect he must have transferred it all to his son. He must have had reservations about handing over all his property so he had kept that small flat in his own name. It's served him very well in his last years. He had a sweet, newly-wed life there. It shows that you should never hand over everything to your children while you are still alive.'

'So the apartment is his only legacy?'

'I hear that before it became a legacy, they sold it. When he had the second stroke and the two households were joined up, they didn't think it was likely that he would ever go back there or that the flat was likely to become more valuable if they hung on to it. So they quickly sold it off. It was just as well. One never knows what kind of petty troubles and trials can await you over some meagre legacy with such things as inheritance tax or division of property.'

Good heavens! To have sold off our flat! Who did that? Who could sell off my flat without my consent? Have you ever heard anything like it in the whole wide world? Songnam-*dek* sprang to her feet. She was determined to go to Jintai's mother at once and reason with her. She was restless and her fists clenched and unclenched itching to grab hold of that white and delicate neck of hers with its shiny gold chain, and shake it wildly as she argued with her. But when she thought about the wicked mouths that had been gossiping about her and the grotesque rumours she had heard just outside her door her feet were not willing to move. Her whole body trembled and she was afraid of the noise outside. I must get it sorted out, of course I must. Do they think I will just put up with it and hide in here as if I was already dead? Too afraid of the noise outside, yet at the same time trying to embolden herself, she was floundering even before she came face to face with them. Outside the din of chatter continued.

'Mirim's mum, would you like to go to the *ddok*-house? What about if we ordered about two *mal* of *injolmi*?'

'No, that's too much. Who would eat all that much *ddok* . . . We can order it by phone. By the way, that's the fried fish for tomorrow. Put it out in the backyard. If you leave it here it will disappear in no time, like everything else. Pork slices will do to put on the table for now. What? Even that's all gone? What an amazing appetite they have! Well, it looks as if we will have to dress some more vegetables for tomorrow.'

'It's not even an outside grave. Do they really need all that food when it is only a crematorium?'

'Of course. It doesn't make any difference. You can't send the guests away hungry even if it is only a cremation, can you?'

'By the way, seeing they are so well off, why couldn't they have had a burial? It is not really good enough for the reputation of the family, is it? How can you cremate your parents?'

'Nowadays if you need a burial you don't even have to arrange it beforehand. The cemetery is quite handy. It's no problem to get a grave site. The thing is that the old man left word asking for cremation, I think. Do you remember how his wife died while his son and his family were in America? When he was organizing the funeral with his two daughters, he seems to have had many thoughts. Apparently he insisted on having her cremated saying that in the future he could not see children still committing themselves to care for the graves of their ancestors. His daughters couldn't prevent it, so it was a cremation. He must have been turning it over in his mind. Apparently he saw no comfort in being buried alone under the earth, so he insisted on being cremated too. He must have fancied that with his wife turned into smoke he ought to be as well, so that he could join her.'

'Of course it is painful for children to cremate their parents but to be filial you have to carry out their wishes, don't you?'

Songnam-*dek* quietly crumpled to the floor. She fancied she could hear, as if from far away, a 'phew' of air being released as the outrage and determination in her heart collapsed. When at last they had all gone she felt miserable and drained as if she herself was a deflated balloon. To say that the old man had wanted to be cremated and had even requested it in his will was a blatant lie. It was true that on his insistence his wife had been cremated, but he had done that in his outrage over his son, who on hearing the news of his mother's death, instead of coming back from America had escaped his duty by phoning his father to tell him that he was sending a small sum of condolence money. The old man had told Songnam-*dek* about it. He did not try to hide from her how close he and his wife had been, and he had told her, with emotion, of how his heart was pierced when he thought of the dreadful heat she must have suffered when her body was put into the stove. She also remembered him saying that he intended to invite the homeless spirit of his wife into his grave and apologize for his cruelty to her and comfort and care for her. If you heard him talking about the dream that he often had in which, with her forehead sizzling with fire or her clothes in flames, she leapt up and down crying out how hot it was, it was obvious how deeply he regretted having her cremated. To suggest that a man like that had requested cremation was sheer nonsense. Besides, she knew that between the time of the second stroke and his death he had never recorded consciousness clearly enough to express any wishes. She herself was the one who had informed the family of his approaching death.

But who would believe her now even if she told them? As the friends of Jintai's mother said, she was a simple woman, but the circumstances became quite clear to her now. At last she perceived the sort of intricate plot in which everyone except herself was taking part. It was about to obliterate every trace of the master who until two days before had reigned over the house filling it with weird mutterings and a terrible smell of shit but with absolute power. There would not be the slightest problem in turning to nothing the promises made between herself and Jintai's mother. By involuntarily stepping into the cog-wheels of a wicked plot that mercilessly wiped out things that were of no use to them, she lost her substance and was squashed as flat as if she had been thoroughly trampled on. She remained for a long time in that state. Perhaps the speed of her abandonment had been too fast. There still lingered a numbing sense of betrayal but quite unexpectedly she felt at peace.

That night she slept well. In the morning, she changed into white clothes and without asking anyone's permission, she got on board the minibus for the funeral. Jintai's mother, still refusing to eat, received the visitors' condolences and comfort and drew much attention to herself. Her friends supporting her on either side, in front and behind, fussed around saying that she had better call at the clinic and have an injection to give her some strength or there would be a double funeral, but she gave a dignified shake of the head as she got into the car. Some of the guests whispered to one another that it was wonderful that even in these days there should be such filial daughters-in-law, while others looked at her with stupefied faces as if they were watching the performances of a popular actress. Even during the ceremony itself the central character was Jintai's mother rather than the dead man. To distract people's attention her sisters-in-law were busily keening as they hugged the coffin, but her position as the chief character did not suffer at all. Her face, drained of blood, was like wax, and as she crumpled like a white handkerchief into the lap of her husband another commotion arose. Probably thinking that she was overacting he made a little speech in her defence.

'My wife has been taking care of my father with such extreme devotion that his death was a great shock to her. It is not surprising if she goes down with exhaustion. All through the last ten months she has waited on his toilet herself, you see. To make it worse she has such a fastidious nature. She can't do anything rough. So you can imagine what suffering she must have endured.'

When they heard this the guests were even more deeply touched and were slowly nodding their heads. Songnam-*dek* felt so ashamed that her face was aflame. In the carriage she alone was a genuine mourner and she felt nervous and insecure. Lest her identity be discovered she contracted herself as best she could and concentrated on staring out of the window. Unsightly buildings, people standing abstractedly, people walking alertly, people desperately hanging on to buses, motorcycles piled high with loads like mountains winding in and out of the traffic, traders shouting their heads off, a beggar with his crippled legs showing like the roots of waterlilies as he pleaded for alms, women carrying their wares on the top of their heads and men with packs on their backs . . . How long she had been cut off from the sight of such people pursuing their varied lives? As if starved she watched them to her heart's content.

Apart from the annexes of stores and lavatories, the place consisted of two major parts. One was the crematorium itself with a tall chimney. Inside, it was grey in colour, and despite the brilliance of the spring day outside, damp and chilly. Here some hearses waited their turn. Supposedly, simple religious ceremonies could be conducted here, but except for the five iron doors of the stove on one wall there was nothing else to suggest such matters. It had an air of desolation as if it was some construction that had been left unfurnished.

Parallel with it stood another building divided into two sections, one a refectory and the other a waiting-room. The two were linked by a concrete path with a roof over it. On either side were beds of yellow soil in which there wilted some European species of flowering plants grown in a greenhouse and transplanted here but not cared for. The refectory was filled with a strong odour of food. It was early for lunch but some families had already opened up their containers and were serving out on plates of silver foil such things as dressed vegetables, fried slices of fish or bean-curd cooked in soya sauce. A man with flushed face was pulling the top off a bottle of *soju* with his teeth. A woman, solacing a young mourner with puffed eyes, saying that the dead are dead but the living must eat, had moist lips with chilli powder on them suggesting that she had already had her fill. One could hardly believe the substance rising from the chimney like a feathery cloud was that of some person burning, nor could one believe it was the refectory of a crematorium. It did not seem to be appropriate in the first place to have a dining-room in a crematorium. There were people voraciously eating, loud voices calling for more food to be brought, children pushing each other around as they ran or played about, the sounds of voices calling for the lost, the smell of *kimchi* . . . It was like a wedding reception, running much later than planned, in a country village. Now and again a young man, a member of the bereaved family, with a cloth band on the sleeve of his coat, could be seen, looking worn out like a bridegroom, though when he smiled he did so with more caution than a groom.

The waiting-room where families gathered before the coffins were put into the furnace was crowded and noisy, bustling with people looking anxious, like a long-distance bus station. They frequently went to and fro between the waiting room, where the coffins were laid out in order, and the refectory, and depending on which one it was, they swiftly switched their expressions. From the direction of the crematorium came the incessant sound of crying and of Buddhist invocations. Here even those who kept their mouths closed seemed draped in grief. The sight, now and again, of mourners nodding off, worn out after sitting up all night, was slightly embarrassing.

Jintai's mother, still unable to hold herself up, was made to lie down on one of the forms in the waiting-room. Where she lay there was an air of calm, peace and dignity like a neutral zone between the funeral area and the dining-room. Indeed, the two differed so radically that it was just as well there was this neutral zone. Those who were not so skilful at quickly shifting their expressions hung about this filial daughter-in-law, their faces wearing cloudy expressions that varied from a vague smile to an equally vague look of concern. Even people who were not at all related to her could not pass by without looking long at her and expressing their concern and respect. It showed how deeply ashamed of themselves they were that their grief fell so far short of hers. To every eye, her calm peace and dignity appeared as the noblest form of a sorrow purified.

Her husband coming from the crematorium with an expression of impatience felt her forehead and said, 'What a weakling you are – I didn't expect you to be so helpless . . .', as he clicked his tongue. Then he bent low as if to turn over her loose hair and whispered in a sharp tone. 'There's a long, long way to go. Fancy, even the dead have to wait in a queue.'

'Use some money!'

Their conversation, like arrows, hit with precision each other's minds. He slunk away towards the crematorium. At last they heard that it was their turn. The others tried to persuade her to stay put but she staggered to her feet as she asked in a fading voice how the wife of the eldest son could refrain from offering her final farewell? When she saw the coffin her sorrow renewed its strength and she started to wail. With her tears all used up, her crying was more like hysteria than an expression of sorrow. As the coffin was wheeled away to the furnace she broke into another fit of hysterics. She leapt after the coffin as if she would follow it into the furnace. They separated her from it by force while the staff quickly pushed it through the door. When she saw the door shut and a red light came on she passed out, her limbs twitching in a fit. Her husband let out a scream, Jintai and Jinsuk broke into tears, and a young male relative lifted her on to his shoulder. She was laid out on one of the forms in the waiting-room, her limbs were massaged, and drops of wine were slipped into her mouth.

In short, there was a big commotion until finally she opened her eyes.

'Where am I? I am sure I am dying.' Her lips twitched as she uttered these words. Her friends made a fuss and suggested that the best thing would be to take her to the hospital for an injection and then let her have a good rest.

'Of course – she should have done that in the first place,' they said. When he saw no one disagreed with the idea, her husband ordered a car to be brought, and took his wife over to it, holding her up. Jintai and Jinsuk went with them. On the family's departure, everyone's face showed a sense of relief. Some of the more dignified visitors sneaked off one by one in their private cars, and those who remained opened the bottles of coke or *soju*. There were calls for food, 'Is there something to bite with the drinks?' One or two food containers were opened.

Songnam-*dek* remained standing alone and watched the iron door. It looked just like the door of the rubbish bin at the flat where she used to live. Once you have lost your usefulness, she reflected, you are no better than rubbish, to be thrown away. She remembered an occasion when she had thrown a fruit knife into the bin with the peel. The old man had insisted on being taken down to the basement where the rubbish was kept. He rummaged through it for half a day and eventually retrieved the knife. His body smelt terrible. It had been hard work to bathe him and wash all his clothes, but how proud he was as if he had achieved something great. She was now carrying with her the sum of money that he had saved from his monthly allowance and given to her. Last night she had made a money-belt of cloth to put it in, and wearing it round her stomach she felt as if she was full even without food. While she was carried away with these thoughts the red light on the iron door suddenly went out. She did not know what that meant but her heart missed a beat, as at the moment when the old man had passed away.

From a narrow passage by the wall with the iron gates someone called the family name. She started to look around, but none of them was there except herself, so feeling rather scared she walked up to where the name had been called. The remains were there already, though strictly speaking they were more a pile of ashes than remains. All that was left on a wheeled tray was something like the remains of a bonfire that had burned well and was now dying out – some pink remnants of fire and white, feathery ashes.

That was all. A member of the staff in a faded blue uniform addressing her as 'granny' asked her, as if suspicious, whether she was the one to take it. She nodded in her confusion. An ordinary-looking man started sweeping the charcoal-like remains with an ordinary hand brush into an ordinary metal pan. As she watched his act of sweeping, not different in any way from everyday sweeping, she felt peace settle into her mind, unlike the fear she had felt at the beginning. She was pleased that she had seen it. She also felt the residue of her uncertain feelings towards Jintai's mother and her own somewhat wistful idea that there was some reckoning to be made dissolving cleanly away without trace. The man who had taken the sweepings somewhere in to the back returned after a while with a white casket with a strap attached to it. She was about to wave her hand saying she would not like to have it hung round her neck when the old man's daughter and her husband came running up to receive it.

When she was left alone, instead of going towards the refectory she slipped out. She asked several people how to find a bus stop for Songnam that would require only one change. To get there would mean a long walk. One person told her it was within the minimum fare for a taxi, six hundred *won*, and another told her that it would cost at least fifteen hundred. It did not matter whether it was six hundred or fifteen hundred. She had never had a taxi so it did not give her any idea of how far it was. But, anyway, she was confident in her ability to walk. With no heavy load on her head, 100 *li* would not be too difficult. It was true, she had been living rather too comfortably lately, but her old walking habits soon revived. As she regained her confidence, unaware of herself, her buttocks were wagging vigorously. When she became aware of it she remembered the bizzare chatter of the women the day before. 'Bloody bitches! – Being comfortably off, all that wagging your buttocks means to you is doing it in bed. How would people like you ever understand the nature of my buttock-wagging, the rhythm of a real tough and healthy life?' It expressed her scorn of them – the only way she could express it. Even without any weight on her head, her habit of shaking her buttocks revived, but not the bad language.

Will they be looking for me at Jintai's? she wondered. Even if they did, it would be no more than looking round for a dog that had gone off in search of its former master, I suppose. Above all, when she thought of taking off her money-belt and giving it to her son she was happy and became excited. What a good job she hadn't told him about the flat. Had he had great expectations, great would be his disappointment, but that was not the case and he would be only too pleased to see a big sum of money. But I must not give him all of it, she decided. I must leave some for myself to start trading again. Soon it would be the season for pickled garlic. Ten packs of a hundred garlic heads are as much as I can carry on my head, and I tried to walk off with a flat. Forget your position in society and you'll be punished, as they say. But as for that flat, it is something that she knows, I know and Heaven knows. How could anyone cheat me so smartly and get away with it? – that bitch! May Heaven punish her!

She thought she would feel relieved only if she could hurl grosser swear words at Jintai's mother, but after three years of repressing herself in her efforts to keep up with the dignity of that family they did not come easily. Indeed, she spat loudly and hastened her steps. As for the swearing, there was no hurry, for there would be time enough for that, but the longing to see her son and his wife and her grandchild that she had endured all this time like torture now went ahead of her, hastening her steps, so that her buttocks shook even more wildly.

# WHY THE SILKWORM DOES NOT LEAVE ITS COCOON

Yoon Chongmo

ONCE again I walk up to the kitchen window. A flight of stone steps leads down to the back alley. To its right lies a long stretch of mulberry bushes and on its left is the mud-brick house sitting with its back towards us.

It may not be much but I love my house and don't envy those with grander ones. I look down at the mud house squatting there like a chrysalis, of which the part that first catches your eye is the concrete chimney that rises from its mud walls.

Each morning as I rubbed the sleep from my eyes and looked out of this window there was always smoke rising from it, a morning message that all was well there. Now, it's only a black hole like a gaping jaw with no wisp of smoke. Round the corner a group of pots and jars huddle together shivering in the cold like a group of abandoned children. The tallest of them, originally a shrimp-sauce container, would be filled with charcoal collected from the oak-wood fire. Another would contain dried ferns and wild herbs from the previous spring waiting to be taken to the market for the Moon Festival of the first month . . . .

A dream from last night comes back. The old woman was calling me in the way she used to when she was alive, in her deep voice. I was telling her, 'She came, granny! She has been!' I had opened wide the front door and gone out but I was this side of the kitchen window and she was out there on the hill path, disconcerted as she looked down across the road. On the road, a woman was coming nearer. It was her daughter . . .

When I awoke it was already dawn. I realize now that it is the third day after the old woman's funeral. I remember her daughter saying that she would come back to sort out her belongings on the third day. I see someone coming down the path by the mulberry bushes. I catch a glimpse of a woman flickering behind them . . . Is it her? A woman in a long padded skirt walks across the hill path. It's only the woman from the rabbit shop.

In a ditch that skirts the mulberry bushes on the right-hand side of the hill path I can see water that had run down from our sewage, frozen thick like the scales of a carp, and where it had spilt over on to the road making it a sheet of ice, there is a layer of sawdust that granny had sprinkled over it.

'Look here! What do you mean by leaving the path in this state? Do you want to see an old woman fall over on her way to the well?' How she used to torment me when I first moved in . . . 'Wherever she's from, what right does she have to come and settle down just above my house?' On the day when I unloaded my belongings feeling as if I had been banished, how sad and disheartening were her unreasonable accusations! Even though the president of the Women's Association, who had called in on a friendly visit, consoled me by saying in an undertone, 'Don't let her upset you. It's her nature. She's tough and swears like anything, so that even the old men are no match for her,' I was already far too upset. I came here because I hated the world and meant to build a house high up on the slope of the hill away from them all but I had ended up as the closest neighbour of that isolated house. That year, when autumn and winter had passed and it was spring, how severely had she reprimanded me for half a day for leaving the vegetable plot unattended.

'Look here,' she said. 'What do you mean by neglecting the land like this? It's full of weeds, and when they come to seed, are you going to let them just fly on to other people's land?'

At that time my heart was like an inflamed scar. I was such a nervous wreck that a speck in the wind could set off a headache.

'Granny, leave me alone,' I pleaded. 'It's because there is no man in the house . . .'.

'Nonsense,' she said. 'Were you a prostitute or a *kiseng* in Seoul? . . . This is only a tiny piece. Even if you only peck at it, you can go over it all in half a day. Get busy at once, can't you?'

'Oh, granny, why do you pester me like this? It's my bit of land. Whether I want to dig it or not is my business . . .'.

'I see. The way you let the land go wild tells me something about your state of mind. You have left your husband . . .'.

'That's right. I had my husband taken away from me. What do

I care about the state of the land? I came to a country village as a refuge in case they took my child away as well. What do I care about a bit of garden plot? I am a woman who has been hit by a severe frost. I can't be bothered with anything at all . . .'

The day after I had exploded like this, she fetched from the village an old man, Mr Koo, and made him plough the land with an ox. And then as she sowed the seeds of spring-onions, lettuce and crown daisies that were to provide my basic supply of vegetables she spoke to me tenderly as if she had undergone a personality change.

'The worse you've been treated the harder you must try to keep busy. Think of your child. When you decided to build a house for yourself it was because you had set your heart on living on with her, wasn't it? So put your heart into looking after it. Walk about the garden, back and front, pull out weeds and plant flowers. Go to the hill and dig up some *durup* roots. Think about how to prepare tasty meals for her. There are lots of people who don't have even that much comfort in their lives.'

The wind from the hills, after biting hard at the walls of our house, rushes on to her's and rampages on the slate roof, blowing like bellows. Dry stems of gourd vine, bleached white, resist with all their might but in the end they are whisked away towards the mulberry trees. I can still hear her saying, 'A slate roof is too steep and slippery for gourds. To grow well they need soft nest of thatch.' When the vine had climbed its wooden pole and reached the roof, and its fruits were dangling along the edge of the eaves, she would go out with an A-frame slung on her shoulders and come back with a load of cut grass which she spread out on the roof.

'Marrow flowers open in the morning and gourds in the evening,' she said. 'Did you know that? In the old days, when clocks were scarce, the women started boiling the barley for supper when they saw the flowers were fully opened.' Flowers that open in the evening . . . as I saw them, pale and white, I was reminded of my womb opening up every night by itself. Sorrowfully I looked up at the moon, my moon, but it kept running further away from me. Hiding my own sorrow, I asked her, 'What do you want to grow gourds for? There are so many other things you can use instead these days?'

'Huh, you come from Seoul but you know nothing. Wait till they are nicely ripe and take them to market. People from Seoul who are keen on so-called "gourd-craft" or folk art come after them like a flock of crows.'

Ah, her and her money . . . living on her own . . .

After such exchanges I would be more preoccupied, when she came round with a bowl of tender vegetable gourd, sliced and dressed tastily with condiments, with the thought of why she sought so desperately every possible means of making money, rather than savouring the delicacy she brought for me. I never saw her buying clothes or even as much as a piece of salted fish for herself. Yet her continued determination to save money . . . There was a time when, on learning that she had made clear her wish to be buried in the village cemetery, I thought that being on her own she was saving up for the time when she would be old and ill. But when she injured her back and was suddenly laid up, it turned out that she had no money even to pay for a doctor.

'I ought to get up. I am going to the ginseng plantation next spring so that I can pay you back the money you gave the doctor . . .'.

The wind, after flailing the mulberry bushes, is now thrashing her empty house. Hadn't she said that she came here more than twenty years ago as a labourer at the flax plantation, and then settled down? She stamped out mud bricks one by one and built the hut herself. The proof of her living here vividly remains but now the house is like someone who has been beaten to death and abandoned in a field. Yes, the husk of that old woman . . . perhaps it is the cocoon of that woman who lived through a whole series of chaotic afflictions and still had to live on. Like silkworms that constantly produce thread to bind themselves up, human life also is a process set towards its final confinement, the grave, as it produces an endless yarn of human experiences which gradually enclose it into a tomb. Probably that is why her spirit can't easily leave the place even after her death. Trapped by the umbilical cord that she had produced, is she still hovering over the edge of the border between this world and the other?

The sound of the wind is like the fierce whistle of a sorceress. All through the night, too, it was thrashing about over the empty fields screaming like a resentful ghost. Probably, that's why I dreamed about her.

I wonder when her daughter will come? The wind, after shaking the slates, is now assaulting the bundles of firewood stacked right up to the eaves, stacks of dead twigs of oak or azalea. 'You have so much already,' I used to say as I pointed up at her stockpile. 'Why do you still have to go out to the hills?'

'There is no work in winter,' she would reply as she took up the sickle again. 'What else have I got to do but gather wood?' In the end she fell and rolled down a slope with the *jigye* frame on her back. Seeing no smoke from the chimney that morning I had gone down to find her lying flat on her tummy unable to budge. The health officer from the local clinic that I called in said that it looked as if her spine was damaged and he could hardly believe that she had got back home with such an injury. I gave her the medicine regularly but she could not get up. When I insisted on hiring a car to take her to the hospital in the town, she was adamant saying, 'What nonsense! I will be up in no time,' and was even annoyed about it. On the sixth day, when I went round with a bowl of bean broth and opened the door, I saw the shadow of the other world around her eyes and lips. Looking exhausted, with a bubbling of thick phlegm, she shook her head as she saw the bowl of food, a faint movement hardly discernible. I saw her shoulder blade move as if she wanted to get her hand from under the quilt. As I turned over one corner of it her emaciated hand reached out close to my knee. It held tightly a damp piece of paper. It was the address of a woman.

'Who is it, granny?' She had told me that she had no husband, no children and was all alone in the world. So who could this be? 'Kim Yong-nai . . .'

'Just once . . . only just once . . .' She appealed in a voice that was fading. The address referred to was that of a town twenty miles away. I immediately set off to find this woman. She lived in a square, flat concrete house by a small stream behind the cattle market. She was about fifty, her hair showing white strands. She shook her head, saying that she didn't know anyone at all living in Kajaegol.

'A tall, thin old lady with a slight limp in her left leg. I understand she is going to be seventy next year.' Feeling at a loss, I described as many of her features as I could think of.

'A limp? I can't think of anyone like that . . . wait a minute, is her name, by any chance, Huboon?'

'I'm afraid I never knew her name.'

'So, what is it you want to see me about?'

'She is ill. She gave me this address and said she wanted to see you just once.' At this her eyes lit up instantly. Her expression seemed to say at last I've got it. Especially I noticed now her firm, prominent jaw like that of the old lady.

'You go back first. I will come along as soon as my husband comes in.'

Is it her daughter? If it is, why doesn't she tell me? The old lady herself told me that she'd never had a child. She used to point to my daughter and say how lucky I was . . . On the way home my mind was in confusion. As I flung open the door I shouted, 'Granny, I've met her. She said she'd come over at once.'

A chilly atmosphere and a sense of calm desolation rushed out to greet me. Could she have . . .? My hand on the door handle froze. Then I saw her eyes staring at me out of the dimness. I gave a sigh of relief as I entered the room. At my footsteps, she must have held even the phlegm from bubbling for I heard her releasing a deep breath, followed by the gurgling sound. While I was getting her medicine ready for controlling the phlegm, her hand reached out for mine.

'Yong-nai . . . my poor child . . .' the words slipped out between the gurgles. 'I left too big a burden . . . to you . . . that . . .' Her eyes, with an age-old yearning in the pupils, searched my face. Kim Yong-nai – so it was her daughter. Then why . . . At that moment I heard the sound of the phlegm choking in her throat. The next moment, she held her hand straight. 'Please let me go back to my children! Please!' These words as they forced their way through the phlegm were as strong as her voice used to be. But it was only for a moment. At the next, her head fell back. These were her last words. Unable to hold out until the evening she drew her last breath. Even so, she was unable to give up her waiting and yearning till the last minute.

Her eyes facing the door were not closed. As I watched over her final moments I thought of my own death. Will my husband be there? Who will let my daughter know? If, despite sending the message no one comes in a hurry, will I also pass away like this before a stranger, or even alone? My only daughter is now twelve. At the time that, on the grounds that I could produce no more children, I was requested to agree to a divorce, she was eight. She had attacked her father. 'I hate you! I hate you, daddy!' After this she ran off to her room and began to bang on the piano. Some time after that her father, who'd been chain-smoking, said, 'My mistress has given birth to a boy. Please try to understand me.

My fault is being an only son in three generations . . .' The day when I was paid the alimony and went back to my mother's home, I held her hand and said, 'You are mummy's daughter. You will always live with mummy.'

Even so, a father is a father. I was told that he was going to the school to see her. I was determined to take her away somewhere beyond his reach. I had a house built in this hamlet some seventy miles from Seoul. The day we were moving in, as we sat in a truck that zig-zagged down a winding country road, my daughter said, 'Mummy, there isn't going to be any such person as a step-father, is there?'

'What a silly girl. To me, you are all that I have.' But what will happen when she marries and goes away? . . . Don't they say, 'No love from the husband – No love from the child? No, that can't be. She will come running to me. She will come and look after me. No, that's not all. She will want to have me living with her even when she is married. After all the love and devotion with which I have brought her up, she will take care of me. It is only natural.

On the way home, after telling the head of the village and the president of the Women's Association about the old lady's death, I saw by one of the mulberry bushes a dog tearing at a large bone. It was in fact the skull of a dog with its teeth in place. How dreadful. Even for an animal, to eat the flesh of its own kind . . . I felt so distressed that I went straight home. After giving my daughter a snack I was standing by the kitchen window when I saw an unfamiliar man coming up the path. Expecting it to be either the husband or a relative of Kim Yong-nai, I ran out.

'I hear Mrs Pak Hubun has passed away?'

'Yes.'

'Can you tell me whether any one has called?' Looking at him again I saw that he was too young to be the husband of the woman. 'You must be her neighbour. If you could tell me if she has had any visitors recently . . .?'

'I don't think so.'

'An elderly man or a middle-aged man of about fifty? Perhaps in the night time . . .?' His enquiry sounded so officious that I felt suddenly tired.

'No one at all. May I ask who you are?'

'I am a police officer from the station in the town. I came out to confirm her death.'

'I'd have thought that was the doctor's job.'

'Well, I have been assigned to her since last year.' As if he was fed up with answering my questions, he opened the door of her room. As he was about to go in he halted, for her eyes were turned to the door as if they were looking at him.

'She did not quite close her eyes,' I explained.

'I see.' He eventually entered the burrow-like room. He was poking about here and there among the sundry objects she had accumulated over the years. From outside I switched on the light which was over the door inside. As revealed by the electric bulb, her body was bluish, like that of someone severely bruised. I wished someone would come quickly so that she could at least be provided with a shroud. The detective inspected the corpse closely for some time before he went out. For some reason his face showed signs of great relief, as of a man who has completed a mission long overdue.

'I understand the village office is going to see to the funeral?' He left after saying a few such customary words. At the edge of the mulberry bushes along the path down which he went, the dog was still holding the skull in his mouth.

I see a woman coming from the opposite direction. It is the mistress of the rabbit shop coming back from a visit to the next village. It is nearly lunch-time and still no sign of the woman yet. I wonder where she is.

She did not arrive that day until the sun had turned the ridge of the western hills, about an hour after the detective had gone. She stood hesitantly on the hill path. I went down and opened the door of the old lady's room. 'She passed away soon after I came back,' I told her. She sat at the head of her mother's body looking down at her eyes for a long time.

'Would you like to close her eyes first,' I said. But it was as if she had not heard. She did not move. Hers was not simply an expression of sorrow or regret but rather of an extreme complexity. Cautiously I told her what the old woman had said in her last moments. At that she let out the word, 'Mother . . .' in a low tone with a deep sigh. Had they for some reason or other been living cut off from one another? Her bleak eyes were looking at me. 'May I ask who you are?'

'I live next door.'

'Do you know how long she's been living here?'

'She told me twenty-three or -four years.'

'After all, she lived so near . . .' Her eyes wandered before turning to me again. 'Did you know her life story?'

'Only that she was all alone in the world . . .'

Her eyes turned to the body of her mother. Tears falling from them were soaking the dead woman's hair. After weeping quietly for some time, she asked me gently, 'Are there many other families with members missing in this village?'

'Families with members missing' . . . When the Women's Association president had used those words, in pointing to someone, I had to ask her what it meant. For someone like me who grew up in an ordinary family, married into a rich one, and apart from being divorced, had never experienced anything unusual, what might be called 'one of the blessed', it was rather an incomprehensible concept. The president had counted on her fingers the names and explained that these elderly women who grew old as they brought up their children single-handed were the ones whose husbands had gone over to the North during the war. Had she been one of them? Why had she made herself out to be a woman widowed young?

'I think there are about five such families . . .' I replied after a long silence. She tidied the edges of the quilt as if the old lady was still alive, and released a deep sigh.

'Do they get along without getting into trouble?'

'I think so, even though they may be very poor . . .' A memory came to me. It had been during the rice-planting season last year. On my way from the market I had been invited to share in the lunch brought out to the fields for the planters. I heard Yamjon's grandmother mumble to herself as she looked at her son who, having finished before the rest, had gone back to the paddy and was smoothing the seed-bed with a plough. 'He's already middle-aged. Older than his father was when he left home . . .' I learned that this was one of them, a 'family with a member missing'. Her husband had gone, leaving her with a boy of three.

'My mother had worked for *Yomeng*, the Communist Women's League. You told me that she had a limp. That explains what happened to her . . .' Women's League . . . my heart gave a bump as it often had when the old lady said something that shocked me. And that bump served as the keynote to many of her doings and habits that I had not understood until then. They all came back to me one after another like a chain. I now understood what her nonsensical confrontation with old Mr Koo had been about . . .

'A short while ago a man from the police came to confirm her death. Does that mean she has always been under surveillance?'

'I can't answer that because I haven't lived with her . . . but I know its true that people in her situation have to report their whereabouts when they go away from their home district even for a short time, and if a lot of handbills are distributed or any slight disturbance occurs in the neighbourhood, they are the first ones to be interrogated. I am over fifty now and I still can't understand this. If mother had committed any crime, it must have been paid for by her time in prison. Why is it that she couldn't come back to her children even after more than ten years there? . . . Probably it was made more difficult for her by my father . . .'

After squeezing the edge of the quilt in her hands as if unwilling to speak, she said, 'My father was a Communist, belonging to the *Namnodang*,' and went on in a quiet voice to tell her life story. Under the Communists he had held an important position in the party and her mother, as his assistant, had worked for the Women's League. She could not remember in detail what her parents thought but she did remember vividly a young woman teacher who, like her mother, used to work for the Women's League. Her main task was to gather the children together under the village tree and teach them songs or tell them stories. One day she put to them a question: 'Listen children, there are two children. One always comes top in the exams and the other one is always at bottom. At the next exam, the first one comes top again and the other at the bottom. Now, tell me, which one is the bad one?'

All the children held up their hands, wanting to give the answer and a boy was chosen. He answered in a clear, brave voice. 'The one who always comes bottom.' The others chimed, 'That's right.' But the teacher shook her head sadly. 'No, children. The one who is always at the top is the bad one.' The children looked sullen and the teacher went on, 'The one at the top must teach the other one all that he knows, so that his friend knows as much as he does. Now, here's another question. Tell me, what must you do for a friend who is weaker than you are?'

'We must help him!'

'That's good children. We are all of the same nation.'

At that time she was twelve. Things went on in this way until one day her father, her elder brother and her mother, having gone out in the morning did not return until late in the night. However busy she was, her mother had never once failed to cook their supper and feed them. They waited and waited for her to return and went to sleep hungry. On the following night she came in very late and woke them quietly. 'Get up and get dressed quickly,' she said and packed some food in a holdall and put a jacket on her younger brother who was five years old.

'Where is daddy? And big brother?' she asked. 'They are waiting for us a long way away. Do hurry up, dear.' They had opened the door and were about to set off when some people rushed in – members of the National Security, with guns. They asked her mother where her husband was and she said she did not know. They prodded her tummy with the muzzle of a gun as they urged her to confess. All her mother said was that she didn't know herself so she was setting off to look for him. Her two younger brothers trembled pitiably but were too scared to cry. After thoroughly searching the house they took their mother away. From then on the three of them were like orphans.

'Still, it was fortunate that it happened at our own house . . .' said the woman as she stroked the tresses of her mother's hair. Suddenly the words of the detective came to my mind, 'An old man or one about fifty years old . . .'

'After that you never saw your father and brother again . . .?' She did not answer to that but continued with her story. Abandoned in the house, the three of them waited for their mother's return. Sometimes they ate and at other times went hungry. In the end they went to the office of National Security as a neighbour suggested, but their mother had long since been transferred somewhere else. The younger ones cried and insisted on going out and looking for their mother, but she did not know where to go. The family of her aunt on the father's side had all disappeared. There was an aunt from her mother's side who had married into a family somewhere in Cholla province but she did not have her address. Her grandfather's house across the river was empty, for her uncles had either fled from the Northern army or joined the Southern. Besides, she did not feel like leaving the house in case her parents returned. Every morning when they woke up her brothers talked about the dreams they had had, their faces gaunt with hunger.

'Sister, I saw my big brother and daddy last night.' As soon as the ten-year-old opened his mouth, the eight-year-old would chime in. 'So did I.'

'They will come, I'm sure they will . . .' she said. During the winter they managed either by begging food from the neighbours or snooping around to beg from the soup tent in the cattle market. After winter came the spring. A boy of her age in the village came and told her that he had seen a body in the silver birch wood that looked like her mother. She went to the wood alone. By a grave, where the trees were thick, was a badly disfigured corpse. It looked as if it had been frozen during the winter and started to decay again, but fortunately it was not that of her mother. The decaying body with its breast hollowed out as if from a gun wound was that of the long-haired teacher who had asked the children what they must do for their friend at the bottom. Frightened, she hurried away. 'The friend at the bottom . . .' The teacher's words seemed to follow her and grab the back of her neck. She got home half-distracted but she could not tell anyone about the body. She was well aware that the world had changed and topics such as the comrade teacher were forbidden.

'It was indeed a troublesome time. Equally confusing were the rumours that spread among the children. Endless numbers of "left-handed" people had been shot and thrown into the reservoir, some said. Others said the "left-handers" who had been hiding in the mountains had crept down and attacked the National Security Office overnight. And some said that a Big-nose riding in a jeep did something awful to a girl gathering wild herbs . . . Such stories were rampant though none of them could be proved.'

'A Big-nose riding in a jeep . . .' This phrase reminded me of one particular summer evening. The old lady had been out on the hill path looking down at the road below in the growing darkness, deep in thought. It was a familiar sight, especially on summer evenings. There had been no work at the hemp plantation so she had been weeding my vegetable patch. When I had finished washing up the supper things, I went down with a tin of beer and some sausages on a tray. I meant to pay her at the same time. It was one of the tins that I kept in the refrigerator for use on sleepless nights, freezing to the touch. Squatting down beside her I opened it. As she took it from me, she broke into an outburst. 'The Big-nosed western bastards – do you know how many of our women they ruined with tempting things like this? The Imperialist villains!' Too surprised for words I just looked at her blankly unable, to the end, to tell her that it was actually made in Korea.

I wondered if I had not misheard her. How could she say such things?

'When my father worked for the party during the Communist reign, there wasn't one single incident of anyone killing or being killed in our village. They all knew that and they talk about it even today. It is true. In our village . . .' As she stressed this point several times, another memory, that of a weird fight at the sixtieth birthday party of Yamjon's grandmother suddenly floated up in my mind as if lifted by a fisherman's hook. It had been the previous spring. The whole village had been urged from the early hours to come and have breakfast at the house of the birthday person. The head of the village had been announcing it through a loudspeaker. It was Sunday. I could not get up early. The old woman had been up to the house twice calling my daughter's name, but I couldn't get up. I had watched the television until the national anthem came to mark the end of the day, and besides that, resentful thoughts about my husband had cropped up through the night to spoil my sleep. I got up late and started washing rice to cook a meal.

'What do you want to cook rice for when there's a feast going on? Come on quick! Bring your daughter along!' Apparently she had been waiting to go with us. Then my daughter said she fancied some *chapchae*. So we went down together. The inner room and the verandah were full of people who had arrived before us, so we had our table in the vinyl greenhouse. Next to us was old Koo, the closest friend of the old woman, sitting at a table with his companions, all drinking merrily. He started teasing her saying, 'Old woman, you came to see me? You couldn't wait, could you?', and at once passed her a cup of wine. She tossed it down her throat at one gulp and picked up her spoon and chopsticks. When the food on our table had nearly gone, the old men at the next table started talking about the husband of Yamjon's grandmother.

'Doksegi – do you think he's still alive somewhere?'

'Who knows? If he was, I wonder if he'd remember it's his wife's birthday today?'

'If he was here, he'd have called in the drummers and made it a grand party.'

'This is grand enough for people like us.'

'It makes you wonder how he could have walked away leaving an almost new bride and a little son behind.'

'He had no choice, did he? After what he'd done . . .'

'True, he was a bit over-active.'

'What about the people who worked for National Security? They were all the same.'

At this point, the old woman put down her spoon with a bang as she joined in the argument. 'The war was made by the Japanese bastards and the Big-nosed buggers. I know all about it. The Japs stirred up MacArthur, to sell their weapons. We were tricked, we didn't have to go to war!'

Koo shouted, 'That bloody woman, talking her nonsense again!' She was not deflated. 'Come on, you old devil, let's hear about what you did for the National Security!'

'I never did anyone any harm!'

'Nor have I!' They croaked at each other 'No.' and 'Nor,' for a while until she sprang to her feet. The leg that visibly limped when she carried things on her head or on her back in the *jigye* was nimble enough as she hopped over to Koo and grabbed him by the front of his jacket. The old man hit at her arm as he repeatedly cried, 'Crazy old thing, crazy old woman.' With her hand still clenching the front of his jacket they began to roll over. Still nobody bothered to separate them. On the contrary, the old men were laughing as they said, 'They are throwing a fit again!' Embarrassed and not knowing what to do I had taken my daughter away.

'Perhaps because no lives had been lost in the changes of power, the villagers were kind to us. They looked after the paddies my parents had farmed and brought in sacks of rice and barley for us.' The woman slowly went on with her story. 'Just the grain was not enough to keep us going. I had to give up school, but my brothers carried on . . .' When her maternal uncle returned after the War he wanted them to live with him but his wife waved her hand in rejection saying, 'You never know what problems might come from taking them under our care . . .' The woman herself, even though she had been young had not liked the idea of becoming attached to her uncle's family. As long as there were the village people who never left them out when there was any festivity or big event and made sure they had their share of the food, she was confident that they would survive. Looking back, she thought it was not so much her sense of duty as the elder sister that had seen the three of them through their hardships, as rather the concern of the villagers, all of them.

'As I grew more sensible I set about earning some money. I sold steamed sweet-potatoes or maize and sometimes I worked in an apple orchard. Looking back it seems a wonder that young as we were we managed so well . . . What frightened us more than the hardships was . . .' They had often been visited by the police, not to bring them news of their mother, but to put questions to them. 'Are you sure your father hasn't been?' or 'How did your brothers pay their school fees?' or 'How did you manage to buy that mosquito net?' and so on . . . Then they would say, 'That's OK then. But if your father or your brother do come home at any time you must report it to the village office or the Home Guard Office, or you will be punished . . .'

'Because we managed to get by without starving, they wanted to know how we did it. They threatened us that if we did not report anything that happened we'd be punished . . .' Every evening she was in torment feeling that her father might turn up. What sort of punishment would fall on her if she did not report it? What would become of her father if she did?

'However, time passed so fast. While I was living a busy life, sometimes squatting in the fields pulling out weeds all day under the scorching sun or scrabbling around in other fields after the harvest to glean a few radish leaves or small sweet-potatoes, I became twenty, fully eligible for marriage. Through an arrangement made by my maternal uncle I was married in a simple ceremony to the second son of a family as poor as our own. It was on the condition that he'd come and live in our house with my younger brothers. The house having been lived in only by children was in a mess and greatly in need of repair. My husband did the repairs and improved it. He was a kind and energetic man and did a lot for the boys' education. The elder one went only as far as middle school, but the younger one went on to finish high school. Both of them were good and never went astray . . . Now they are independent and doing quite well for themselves. The elder one has a clock shop in Pusan and the younger one . . .'

She had been married for some years. The elder of her two boys had gone away hoping to learn some skill, while the younger was in his last year at high school. One day, late in the morning, her maternal uncle, who lived on the other side of the river, came to see her. Her husband happened to be out helping to build a dam. Her uncle didn't want to go inside. He sat on the wooden verandah and called, 'Yong-nai!' and then fell silent for a time. He had never been like this before so she was baffled and felt a premonition. She wondered if he had some news of her father, either that he had called, or he was dead.

'I can't understand it, but the one I had always expected was my father, and not mother. Perhaps I had given up the idea of meeting her again because I had seen her being taken away, or because, after seeing the body of that woman teacher I believed that the same fate must have fallen on her. Even on the night after I was married I kept thinking that father might turn up . . .'

Her uncle opened his mouth at last. 'Yong-nai, . . . sister has been to see me and left again early this morning. She is out of prison. She was crying ever such a lot, saying she had made you suffer far too much, and admired the way you have managed with your two brothers . . .' So the news was not of her father but of her mother! Then her going away again! There were so many things she had wanted to tell her – and she had gone away just like that! For the first time in her life she strongly blamed her uncle. 'Why did you send her away? How is it possible! How could she go away so lightly without even calling here? Uncle, please, let's go and look for her. Let's go now!'

'He comforted me and explained, "Even though they are out of prison, people like your mother are not free. Your brothers are still not old enough to look after themselves and there is always the danger that this connection could hinder their future, so I suggested that it would be better for her to go away without seeing you all . . .". What right did he have to say such things to mother and send her away like that? My brothers had made up their mind from the beginning that they would never want to be civil servants . . . oh, dear. I went out to search for her. I went to uncle's house, to the bus station, all over the place, but in vain. She had disappeared without trace, to a place where we would never find her. And after all she was here all the time . . . only a short distance away . . .!' The woman was dabbing her moist eyes with the back of her hand. The chilly face of the old lady seemed to be moist as well. As I swallowed deep sighs, the woman spoke again. 'I didn't feel like this while I was living with my brothers but as I had my own baby and became a mother myself I understood my mother's love for us afresh. In all likelihood, it was because of us, her three children, that she was caught in that way. You see, she could have run away taking her eldest son, but she had turned back because she could not leave us behind . . .'

Anyway, she had abandoned the hope of finding her and gone on living her own life. She had even put away the thought of her father. She had given birth to her children and her brothers had grown up. Then a few days before the wedding of the elder of the two brothers, she received by post quite a large sum of money. The sender's name was not given, but instinct told her it was from her mother. There was no way in which she could find the address. Her mother had thoroughly sealed off the ways of finding it.

'Ever since, she's been sending me money without fail on occasions such as marriages or my brothers' birthdays. She even found out the birthday of my child . . . Without fail . . .' Yong-nai looked hard into my eyes as she asked, 'Do you think mother was paying what she thought was a debt to me for bringing up my brothers? If she thought like that she was wrong. I did not bring them up alone, did I? My husband and the village people, all of them . . . Even if I did, it is only natural. They were not strangers, they were my own brothers. We are quite well off now without any worries about feeding the family . . .'

I understood it all. She used to gather wild herbs and take them to market, take on any kind of job anywhere. When she saw a patch of empty soil on a path between the paddies she would plant beans or maize, and gather it in with great efficiency, chestnuts fallen in the wood and even acorns. It was all a means of money for her daughter. Alas, when she brought ginseng roots that she had thinned out of the plantation, why hadn't I bought any? I had complained that they were too small. Why didn't I buy her a bowl of sausage soup when I saw her on market day squatting down behind such things as dates and beans? Knowing perfectly well that money was too precious to her for her to buy herself even a bowl of noodle soup, why did I leave her, making excuses about catching the bus and so on? When I went to the village office, and saw her limping into the post office, why had I treated her with such indifference?

Yong-nai was looking down into her mother's eyes. Under the dim electric light, perhaps because of the shadows, they looked as if they were weeping. She went on endlessly looking into these eyes without closing them. Probably she could not bring herself to accept the fact that her mother had passed away without exchanging a single word or giving her a chance to tell her the story of how hard it had been to survive.

'Mother,' she said, 'I hear that now even the Complicity Law has been repealed. So why didn't you think of coming back . . .' At last she broke down and sobbed bitterly as she continued to hold tightly the edge of the quilt. I said, 'Don't you think we ought to wrap her in a shroud?' and went to the door. Outside, the old man, Mr Koo, stood abstracted in the darkness.

The wind finally blew down a bundle of firewood from the pile. Even the chimney seems to be shaky. When spring comes, the house will be pulled down. I see now that it is not her cocoon. It is more like the shabby clothes that she had begged and put on. He real cocoon made of her own juice is not her queer behaviour nor the rough personality she had shown. It is her daughter and her sons . . . her own flesh and blood. That is not all. Her cocoon is all these put together.

A woman is walking down from the other side of the mulberry bush. With her are two men in mouse-grey overcoats . . . It is her. I see she has been to the grave with her brothers . . . They are about to turn into the hill path. In my dream last night, the old woman was waiting for her children to come up like that . . . Can she now at last leave that mud hut with a light heart?

The funeral had taken place immediately. Yong-nai had offered to summon her brothers and take her mother's body back to her home, but the head of the village said it couldn't be done, as the funeral had been officially assigned to him. Young men from the village got the communal bier out from its shed and bore the coffin to the communal burial ground in the wood behind the village. Mr Koo, who acted as the chief mourner, wept, cooing like a wood pigeon all the way as he followed the bier. The old man who at her request would go dragging an ox as far as that deserted patch of land deep in the wood to plough it, and when, in disagreement, would fight her brandishing his fists . . . What, I wonder, was the significance of that close relationship between her and this old man who, I understand, had helped with National Security?

'Mummy, aren't you going to give me any dinner?' It is my daughter calling from behind me.

'Yes, your majesty, of course I will.' I turn round with a bright, big smile. There stands my daughter, the cocoon of my egoism, with a pure face regardless of my selfishness, smiling cheerily.

# THE POET OF WONMI-DONG

Yang Guija

EVIDENTLY they see me as reasonably satisfactory for a girl of seven, but I am more than that. To say that I know all about the ways of life may sound big-headed but it is true that I have a clear insight into how things are in my own family and enough sense to see through the minds of people in the village. It is not so surprising for, to tell the truth, I must be eight or nine years old.

At the time I was born, I am told, I was such a poor thing that they did not expect me to live, so from day to day they kept on putting off the registration of my birth. That is the reason for the uncertainty about my age, but it was a good job that eventually they did get me registered, even if it makes me a seven-year-old. I can understand my mother's hopes at that time that I would not survive. My father's not too bad, but she always snarls at me. I don't even mind so much her perpetual moaning about how I was unexpected, quite out of the blue, but she decided to have me, hoping against hope, and I turned out to be just another of those hateful daughters.

I understand her, not because I am particularly mature for my age, but because I can see how things are at home. By the time I was born my parents already had no fewer than four daughters, ranging from the eldest, a fully-grown maiden of more than twenty to the youngest in her last year at High School. My mother, then forty-three, did not realize she was pregnant until she was three or four months gone. It was after consulting famous fortune-tellers here and there that she decided to have me for they unanimously assured her that it would be a boy. In a situation like that, as if it was not enough to come out with a hole, I did not slip out easily either but turned and twisted, almost killing her. So here I am. I can't say a word even if I had ten mouths. But there is nothing for my mother to be proud about either – she keeps changing her mind about my age, eight one day and nine the next. She seems to think I am a blockhead at adding up or taking away but I am not at all. It's as clear as day that she went on hoping I would die until I was well over three.

I don't mean to go on about how badly I'm treated as the ugly duckling, for what I really want to talk about is not trivial things like that but about the poet of Wonmi village. I know that I know a lot but even so I can't explain what poetry is all about. To my rough idea, it was something like uttering a few smart words with downcast eyes on a moonlit night or by the seaside as the waves roll in, but from the way this poet goes about it, it doesn't have to be like that. Besides him there are other characters in our Wonmi neighbourhood. There is the 'Wonmi Singer', the 'Wonmi Beauty', the 'Know-all of Wonmi', and so on. The singer is Mr Um of the Happy Photo Studio whom I call 'Uncle Um', but seeing that he failed to get through even the first round of the national song contest held recently in Buchon, his singing can't be all that good. The local beauty is Nora's mum and I know she must be for she's the only one who uses purple nail varnish and she dyes her hair yellow. The 'know-all' is my mum, I am ashamed to say, ashamed because I know it is an insulting way of describing someone who meddles with other people's business and keeps getting into arguments at the slightest provocation. The Wonmi poet has another nickname – 'Mr Mongdal'. It was Kyong-ja, the beautician at the Seoul Beauty Salon, whom I call 'Sister Kyong-ja', who started calling him that, saying that with his deep-sunk eyes, his unkempt hair standing on end and the dyed army jumper and threadbare jeans that he wears all through the year, when you saw him at night, he made you think of a 'mongdal ghost' which means the ghost of man who has died unmarried. Not only Sister Kyong-ja but everyone else tends to treat him in a rather rude and contemptuous way as if he were a child. The reason, I am told, is that he is slightly queer in the head. I don't know when he started to be like that or how bad he is, but certainly I can see that he is a little different from other people.

He lives in a second-floor apartment of the Mugungwha Housing Complex. On his balcony are a great many plants and no fewer than three hanging bird cages. Inside, the air-conditioner hums all through the day in summer, which is a rarity in our neighbourhood. They are a wealthy family. His father, who practises herbal medicine in the town, has made a second marriage to a younger woman in his old age and is in the middle of enjoying his new conjugal bliss. Mongdal is the youngest son and should have stayed on with his married elder brother, but has moved in with his father, deep in the bliss of his new life. Kohung Auntie at the Golden Estate Agency keeps criticizing this, saying that it is the sort of thing that only an idiot would do, but I can't see why it should be idiotic for a son to live with his own father.

If, as such a man, he has a friend, it is me, the only one. He is twenty-seven – some twenty years older than me, but there is no doubt that we are friends. You will never believe this, but I have another male friend of twenty-seven. Mr Kim of the Lucky Supermarket, next door to our house, is the ward leader of the Fifth Street of Twenty-Third District, Wonmi-dong. He used to be the most manly and interesting person that I knew. There was a time when almost every day I used to sit on a chair under a beach parasol in front of his store and pass the whole day happy in the fun of giggling with him. These days he rarely makes me laugh or hands over a '*ju-ju*' bar or two as he used to do. He has become rather abrupt. I know the reason well enough but what can I do but pretend that I don't? It is because last month my third sister, Sun-suk, suddenly left home and went to stay with my aunt in Seoul. Everyone knew that there were fond goings-on between them. Then recently she became restless, and finally she went off to the city saying she would help her aunt who runs a clothes shop. She had indeed a pretty face. It is not too much to say, as the local people do, that she was 'a dragon that came out of a ditch'. It was a shame for a girl like that to be stuck in a dump like our home. She hated it and was always grumpy.

I really hate to make this known, but my father is a rubbish man. From dawn to dusk he has to poke about with rubbish bins, so he stinks. There is something else I don't like to let out. It's all right with my eldest sister, for she has been married off to a farmer in Yangpyong, but I am embarrassed to talk about my second sister. At first she was a bus conductor, then she worked at a sausage factory and after that was a waitress at a Tea Room. As a twenty-six-year-old maid, she was so frantic to earn some money that she opened up a drinking house somewhere in Gurodong. I went there once and saw a man as tall as a flagpole lying asleep in her only room with his shirt front flung open. As for her, she was lying on her tummy by his side turning over the pages of a magazine. That was enough for me to understand how things are with her.

My mother, and my father, the rubbishman, thought that Middle School was enough education for their daughters to marry with, but for some reason they sent Sunsuk as far as High School. That was asking for trouble. 'As a High School graduate I can't work in a factory, I'd rather be a film actress,' she used to say with a grim expression. Of course, a girl like that could not be contented with Mr Kim's poky little shop.

It may strike you as odd that a seven-year-old, though I am really older than that, should get on with no one but old bachelors, but it is not my fault. All my pals, including Nora, my favourite, started school this year or the year before, and even the younger ones, whom I could put up with if I wanted friends, go to the kindergarten. So when I went out after breakfast there was no one to play with except two-year-old urchins with dribbly noses. Even in the afternoons things were no better, for the children just played among themselves and wouldn't include me in their games. So I became the odd one out and just stalked about. There were cheap kindergartens in our area, and a couple of places where you could have piano lessons, but my mother was adamant. Even families living in one room sent their children to the playschool, making a great din every morning, but I had never had even as much as a dancing lesson. There are plenty of picture books or broken toys lying about the house that my father salvages from rubbish bins, but I am no longer interested in them. I think I must be grown up.

It was in the spring of this year when, feeling like an outsider, I became friends with Mongdal. I was strolling up and down in front of the Lucky Supermarket and casting a wistful glance now and again at Mr Kim hoping he would at some time speak to me. It was then that I noticed Mongdal casting glances at Mr Kim in exactly the same way. He took a crumpled piece of paper from the pocket of his dyed fatigues and hesitatingly wandered up to an empty chair next to me as he smoothed the paper. He sat down, and when he spoke my name 'Jai-suk' I jumped and nearly died of shock. I knew of him as someone 'with a screw loose', and once I had teased him, I admit, calling him to his face,

'Mongdal ghost!' I was so startled I remained with my mouth wide open. His next words staggered me even more:

'You call me a dog, a bastard of a dog, you keep on calling me that . . .'

I opened my eyes round. I had once called him 'Mongdal ghost', it's true, but I can swear to God I never ever called him a dog. So I shook my head vigorously. Whether he noticed it or not, he went on saying, 'You call me a dog, a bastard of a dog, you keep on calling me that . . .'

Even now I can't believe it, but apparently it was a so-called poem. What happened was that Mr Kim, on learning that Mongdal was a poet, had urged him to try and write a good poem. Thus asked, he had struggled with might and main to compose one but in vain. It did not come out as he had intended, so he had copied out one by a famous poet, and he was reading the last line.

'Come on, man. When did I ever call you that, eh?' said Mr Kim teasingly as he tapped him on the shoulder with an expression as if to say 'It does not surprise me.' That was that with him. As for me the shock of it all did not wear off easily. I almost fancied that I must have insulted him by calling him that at some time and had perhaps forgotten. Regardless of Kim's response, Mongdal went about for the next few days reciting to himself the poem of the dog and I made up my mind that I would become friends with him as well as Kim. To be the friend of a poet seemed much more attractive than of the owner of a poky supermarket.

Even so, I did not have the pluck to go about for long with a man who was slightly queer. Besides, with Kim it was always possible that he would offer me a boiled sweet or two or a '*ju-ju*' bar any time when he felt like it while Mongdal was no good in that way. All he did was talk about poems, think about them and want me to remember them with him. In short, poetry was all that mattered to him. When the wind rose, 'the sound that brushed past the blades of grass' made his heart ache. When he saw a nun passing by he would suddenly cry 'Seventeen, or twenty-one buttons imprisoned her.' He could pass the whole day, just reciting pieces by famous poets. That was not all. You could spend hours talking about a particular phrase of a poem you knew, he told me. Of such was a poetic conversation. To be able to do that, he said, he read poems all through the night. After reading and remembering them, lying on his tummy, all night he made poetic conversations the next day.

Take away poetry, and he would be a very lonesome person just like me. During the day he had no other way to spend his time than to stay at home with his youngish stepmother. So he just walked round the village again and again to fill it in. Sometimes when I was sitting opposite to Kim talking about things that were not particularly new, he would slink along and plonk himself down in one of the chairs, his back slightly bent. He seemed to me to cherish a desire, much stronger than mine, to make a friend of Mr Kim. We would sit quite comfortably for a while in the midday heat idling away the time, either reading the newspaper or dozing off until some customers turned up for a glass of cheap wine or some such thing. Then we would quickly vacate our chairs and absently watch Mr Kim fussing about. Whenever Mongdal brought up the subject of poetry, Kim would change it to something else so that he had to shut up and he rarely spoke about it while he was around. Instead it all came to me. I was the sole listener to the incessant poetic conversation of the poet of Wonmi.

Until one particular event occurred, I had preferred to be with Mr Kim. When he slapped my bottom with his huge hand and called, 'Hey, Jai-suk, my little sister-in-law,' I felt sort of good, so that unaware of myself I broke into a smile. Sometimes when I was riding behind him on his motorbike on his delivery calls, the girls on their way to their piano lessons would look at me with their fingers in their mouths as if they were dying from envy. The mistress of Kohung House, whom I called 'Kohung Auntie', knew that Mr Kim was friendly with every chatty woman in the village and doing well from the sale not only of vegetables but fish as well, and she would often say things about my sister Sun-suk with hidden sarcasm, 'All that Sun-suk has are a few good looks. Considering the way things are with her family, well, Mr Kim, the head man of the district, is too good a prize for her.' Well, I can guess what's in her mind. She has a daughter of her own, a year older than Sun-suk, whose looks are a bit irregular and it drives her mad. Nevertheless, she was ridiculing the words of Eunhae's grandmother when she said the other day that she ought to be quick about her daughter's marriage and get someone like Mr Kim as her son-in-law. She replied: 'In this day and age, what do parents have to do with it? Whatever they see in her, her eyes are on higher things than a man like him. She wouldn't let me even mention him. We had an offer, through a matchmaker, from the assistant manager at the Bank, but she wouldn't even consider it. Though it was only a technical one, she has had a year's taste of college life, and I have to say she's very knowledgeable.'

Whenever I hear such words, I feel something itching madly in my throat. The reason for this itch is that I knew yet another secret. This really is a very special one and if Kohung Auntie ever found out, I don't know what she would do about it. The thought of it worries me to death.

Nobody will ever know who Dong-a, her daughter, is in love with. It is something I happened to find out when I went to my friend Nora's house to play with her last spring. Even Nora herself hasn't the slightest inkling so I have to worry over it all by myself. After that, whenever I meet a member of Dong-a's family I get even more restless. I have never breathed a word of it to anyone until now so I am a bit reluctant but I can't help it. Now that I have gone this far I might as well bring it out. Dong-a is having an affair with a rough young man who helps Nora's dad at his shop, Daishin Facilities. It is no ordinary affair. That day last spring when I went to Nora's I could not find her straight away. So I casually walked round the corner of the house and peeped through a window at the side. I saw a man and a woman sitting stuck to one another and behaving in a queer way. Well, Dong-a was bad enough but the man was sweating like mad as he held her head tight in his arms. It was even a bit scary.

I'm wandering from the point for no good reason. Anyway, I think it is rather a pity that my sister has thrown over Mr Kim. He hasn't completely given up hope and whenever he sees me he never fails to ask if she has been home. As for her, on her occasional home visits she never bothers so much as to cast a glance at the Lucky Super. She was like that even before she left. During these visits she sometimes breaks into freshly abusing him saying, 'Ugh, that rascal, shabby as a beggars' foot-wrapper!' Apparently he somehow found out the phone number of my auntie's clothes shop and he rings her up whenever he feels like it – she was gritting her teeth as she told me. Close observation tells me that my sister has recently fallen in love with another man. She's not like she used to be and she changes her clothes anywhere and everywhere flinging off her underwear, and its daintiness catches my eye and puts me in a flutter. If I lay my hands on them or feel them she slaps my wrist and says 'What do you think? Isn't it pretty? You've never seen anything like this, Jai-suk, have you, eh? They are all things I was given.' It seemed queer to me for a chap to make a present of panties all loosely put together with delicate strings, and I hated her even more when she behaved like that. At such times I felt sorry for Mr Kim who did not know what was going on.

There were occasions when Kim's human value seemed to go up through the presence of Mongdal. I was only a child so nobody minded me hanging around under the beach parasols at the Lucky Supermarket but for Mongdal, of the same age as Kim, to hang about the shop doing nothing and sometimes like me noisily sucking a '*ju-ju*' bar was different. The village elders as they passed clicked their tongues.

'They say he wasn't like that at all until he went to college. I don't know all the ins and outs but he was somehow chucked out of it. It's obvious, isn't it, what students are like these days? Then he went away to do his military duty and came back. It was from then on that he became like that. He goes on mumbling poems all the time. It's not like he's gone completely mad. It is very difficult to know what to do with him. It'll be the death of me.' This was what Mongdal's stepmother confided to Mr Kim. She was a regular customer of the Lucky Supermarket. 'It'll be the death of me' was her habitual phrase. 'If only he would go about in some decent clothes, at least to save my face . . . It'll be the death of me.'

While I am on about his clothes, I may as well say that they would be just the thing for the errand boy of the supermarket to wear. As we got bored stiff with sitting on the chairs doing nothing all day we often used to help out with jobs that needed doing. A contribution that could be counted as our own initiative was to sprinkle the ground in front of the shop with a hose. There was no better way to subdue the dust on the badly paved road or to reduce the fierceness of the summer heat. Kim was pleased with our work and when we had finished he would throw us a carton of yoghurt each as if to say 'Cheers!'.

In this way, it came to pass that the number of Mongdal's jobs grew, one by one, extending to such things as cleaning the shop front, piling up the empty boxes in the basement store, and running errands for the drinking guests. It seemed very strange that the larger the number of things he did the more lordly became Mr Kim, while Mongdal grew shabbier and humbler. Kim was not unaware of this, for once I heard him say in earnest, as he embraced his shoulders, 'I am sorry to make a poet like you work like this.

I am sure of your quality as a poet. One day when I am not so busy I mean to give your poems a careful reading. I may look like a nobody but at school I used to write the letters to the soldiers at the front for all of my friends. I was that good at writing myself.'

At that, Mongdal, greatly cheered, would busy himself even washing the chopping board on which fish were headed and cleaned, and trimming the vegetables that lay around. But to this day Kim has never so much as glanced at his notebook of poems. When Mongdal did manage to get hold of him and say that as his own poems were not yet worth reading, wouldn't he rather like to try the work of a well-known poet, offering a crumpled piece of paper, Kim would make all sorts of excuses to get away from him. As he went, while Mongdal was not looking, he would draw a circle in the air over his head with his finger. Unaware of this Mongdal always carried crammed in his pocket crumpled pieces of paper with poems in readiness for Kim when the moment came. At this point, also bored stiff by Mongdal's poetic conversation, I would also leave, following suit by drawing a circle with my fingers over my own head. Whether he was slightly mad or really mad, the poet of Wonmi, unperturbed by all this, carried on calmly doing odd jobs in the Lucky Super as if he were an errand boy.

I want to make it quite clear that until about a fortnight ago, when a certain event occurred, I had secretly hoped that Mr Kim would become my third brother-in-law. I dislike my eldest sister's husband who is a farmer because he's so old, more like a father, while my second sister, whatever she has done, is still officially a maiden. My only chance of getting a brother-in-law lay in the hope that Sun-suk would marry a man like Mr Kim, the district leader. There is also my fourth sister, it is true, who is probably in love with a boy at the place where she works as I notice that suddenly she seems to spend much more time on her toilet. But she has little chance of getting married yet as there are two others before her. If Sun-suk married Mr Kim, it would mean that I could stay put here at the Lucky Super by right. If I wanted to, I could eat even the '*Pangparae*' which is three hundred *won*. When I thought of how all those tastefully displayed biscuits, chocolates and sweets would be within my reach I could not help a cosy happiness spreading within me.

Then, exactly a fortnight ago, it happened, and because of that I have decided to give him up completely, as well as all the goodies at his shop. I may be wrong, but I believe a hundred times over that my decision has been right. I was the sole witness of that incident from beginning to end, but I haven't spoken to anyone about it. For some reason I didn't feel like breathing a word. In this way, which is entirely my own, I have disqualified Mr Kim as a prospective brother-in-law. The other matter required more courage. It was that since that day I have strictly refused to let him slap my bottom and say 'Hey, Jai-suk, my little sister-in-law' and so on. When he did it I pushed him off and ran away. And of course I refused to take the '*ju-ju*' bars that he thrust at me.

It was after ten on an early summer morning when it happened. The quarrel between my mum and dad that had been going on and off all through the day became a proper row by the evening. My fourth sister, who went out to work, rarely came home before midnight, saying that she had been detained for some late-night job. So I had been the only object on which my mother could vent her anger and I had been abused a great deal. The reason behind their row was rather trivial. It started off with my mother nagging him after he had told her how he had found an eighteen-carat gold necklace amongst the rubbish and exchanged it for four bottles of beer with which he had happily wetted his throat on the way home. To cut a long story short, the point of her noisy accusations was that instead of drinking it all up in four bottles of beer he could have put it round his wife's neck – did he think that would have brought him bad luck? The eighteen-carat ring on her finger that had slightly lost colour had been picked up by dad in that way. The thought of what a nice set the two would have made angered her fiercely. A lively argument that led by the evening to vile abuse and a beating from my father, so I had stealthily slipped out of the house, as was usually the case, and was sitting on the chair in front of the supermarket. These quarrels happened frequently and I knew how it would end. Soon, father, having beaten her, would fall asleep and snore. Mother, after squeezing out the last of her tears, would go out to the street dragging her feet and call 'Jai-suk!' as loudly as she could. Only then would I go in, as if unwillingly, get into bed and the morning of an another day was sure to come.

It was about nine o'clock when I went out. Mr Kim was watching the evening news on his black-and-white television in the room at the back of the shop and had not noticed my arrival. I cast a quick glance at the back of a man who put up with an ancient television set, saying there was no need to change it as when he got married his bride would no doubt bring a new one with her, took off my shoes, and folded up my legs on the chair. If I was sleepy, I thought, I could rest my head on the table and doze off for a time. I was rubbing my droopy eyes and shifting my body this way and that. That evening the street seemed unusually quiet. Even the paper shop and the Photo Studio had turned off the lights of their signboards. As if it was a holiday, the Uri Butchers had even pulled down the shutters. The hair salon next to it always had the lights off by nine anyway, as Kyong-ja, the beautician, went home at night. The road that led from the Lucky Super towards the housing estate was pitch dark as it was lined with empty building-sites. A dim light that leaked out from a laundry was a whole block away. Along the unpaved, bumpy road piles of bricks and pebbles lay here and there.

At that moment I heard a noise from the direction of the housing estate – a scream or a moan that comes from a retching. No, I could hardly have heard the sound for I was, more or less, wandering in my sleep. Come to think of it, I am sure I was fast asleep at that moment. Maybe the reason for me thinking I heard a noise in spite of being asleep is because I was looking at my mum and dad who had even followed me into my sleep, still fighting. Anyway, whether the scream that cut the air was dream or reality I certainly heard it. When I started and opened my eyes I saw someone dashing out of the darkness and running desperately towards the shop. Behind him came two men panting for breath, as if they were after a deer that had sprung out of their trap.

It so happened that I was sitting out of the light and so out of their sight. It also happened that there was no one else around the shop. Often, far more people than there were chairs for under the parasols would gather here and drink noisily. They would be mostly labourers on their way home from a building site. There would also be local people who often sat in a group to relax and enjoy the breeze. But none of them was there that night. While I was staggered to be faced with such a situation so suddenly, the escaper ran straight into the shop. Of the two pursuers, one stood in front of it while the other went inside, and I had a chance to observe them more clearly.

'Hey, bastard! Come out of there, can't you!' The man who shouted as he ran into the shop wore a red sleeveless singlet that showed powerful shoulders glistening with sweat. 'Before I smash you up, come out, do you hear?'

The one in front of the shop, breathing heavily as he wiped the sweat from his forehead, held two jackets in one hand. He was wearing a T-shirt and probably because of its sleeves and quiet colour, he looked rather milder than the red shirt.

What was it? Unable to suppress my curiosity, I crept to the side of the shop and peeped through the side-door. The runner had been laid flat, face downwards, by the kicks of the chaser, and Mr Kim was shouting something as he carried away into the room the beer boxes that lay around the victim in case the situation worsened.

'Mr Kim, Mr Kim . . . please help me.' It was just at that moment that these words slipped faintly from the lips of the fallen man. At the same time a foot was pressed harder on his waist.

'Look here, are you a friend of this bastard? If so, do you want a bit of this as well?' shouted the red shirt brandishing a beer bottle. Mr Kim turned white. 'Why, what do you mean? He's nothing to me! I don't want anything to do with it. Both of you, please get out of here and sort it out somewhere else, please.'

At that moment the man floundering on the ground twisted himself and just managed to get up. The face, messed up with blood from his nose, caught my eye, and Good Heavens! it was Mongdal! I recognized his bleached trousers and dyed jumper, and underneath the grim-looking shirt it was undoubtedly Mongdal. I had not been able to see his face earlier because he had run into the shop so quickly.

'You bastard, where are you going to wriggle out? I'm going to beat you up and teach you a lesson.' White teeth flashed as the red shirt roared. Mongdal instantly leapt into the room where the television was making a noise. He knew there was a way out through there. But someone else got there first to block the way. Mr Kim!

'Get out! Both of you! Whether you want to fight or not is up to you but just don't ruin my business!'

The red shirt grabbed Mongdal by the neck. When he saw him being dragged out like a dog, the white shirt spat through his clenched teeth with a squelch. The two men were on fire with drink and their glossy eyes were eerie. I quickly hid in a corner away from the light. I was terrified. I had no idea what I ought to do to help Mongdal, who was now being dragged away. My heart beat so fast that I could not even breathe properly. Yet Mr

Kim didn't bother so much as to look out towards the road once as he tidied up his shop.

It was obvious that of the two men, the one in the red singlet was the more evil. He grabbed a handful of Mongdal's hair, wound it round his hand and dragged him along like a parcel. As his victim squirmed and struggled against it his shins and waist were mercilessly kicked on. By now there were several passers-by who watched them with frightened faces. When he saw the spectators Red Shirt pronounced authoritatively, 'Come on. A bastard like this must be handed straight over to the police. Come on!'

In front of the Golden Estate Agent's lights, Mongdal exerted his last drop of strength and freed himself, but no sooner was he free than he was caught again by his hair and his head bumped a concrete column beside the Office. At the sound of it I shut my eyes. I was choking. I knew that if you went past the Happy Photo Studio and Wonmi Papershop, there would again be an empty space with no glimmer of light, and that it was the last chance to save him. He was desperately trying to stay near the lights of the shops as he was being dragged along. This side of the road was quiet except for one or two people who were careful not to get swept into the row. All they did was to click their tongues at the miserable sight.

'Hurry up, bastard! Let's get to the police, do you hear!'

As the Red Shirt tugged at his hair, Mongdal, unable to stay on his feet, had to crawl on all fours like a dog.

'Why are you doing this to me . . . what have I done? . . . what have I . . .' In front of the bright lights of the Happy Photo Studio, he shook his head in the man's grip as he protested, only to be kicked in the face. At last I shot out. With clenched fists I ran past them like the wind and ran into the Wonmi Papers. Mr Cho, the owner, had left his counting and was stretched out at the warm end of the room watching the television, totally unaware of the turmoil outside.

'They are killing Mongdal!'

For a man of such size he was quick to grasp things. He ran out in a flash, saw Mongdal being dragged along right in front of his shop, and spoke up loudly. 'If he has done something wrong you can call the police. What on earth are you hitting him like this for? Look here, man, let him go.'

At this outpouring in an uncouth Kyongsang dialect, even the thug was slightly taken aback.

'Mind your own business, mister! A sod like this has to be handed over to the police.'

'Rubbish! Look here! Call the police. You don't have to take him there yourself, beating him up all the way. They'll be here in a minute on motorbikes.'

'Look mister . . . this sod . . . do you know him?'

'I know him well – of course I do. This good young man . . . What has he done wrong for you to beat him to death? Tell me!'

Only then did Red Shirt furtively let go of the hair he had been holding. Mongdal moved unsteadily to the side of Mr Cho.

'I haven't done . . . anything wrong . . . I was just walking along . . . when they rushed at me . . . and started hitting me.'

It was unfortunate that Mr Cho took his eyes off them to listen to Mongdal who between his faltering words was spitting out the blood that filled his mouth. One of the spectators standing some distance away shouted, 'Look – they're running away!'

It was true. In the blink of an eye they had raced off. They were already on the road to the housing estate. I could only hear the patter of their footsteps. They were already swallowed up by the darkness.

'We must go after them. We mustn't let them get away with it!' Whenever he had come, Mr Kim was excitedly stamping the pavement. It was a sight to see him jumping up and down as if he would run after them.

'You wouldn't say that if you knew what they were like,' said someone. 'They are . . .'

'Good heavens, they were saying so impressively that they must go to the police, and now look at them running away!'

'So they just picked on him and started beating him up, is that it? We thought he must be really a thief or something. How awful!'

'There's too much light here from the shops. I can see they were going to take him somewhere dark and really thrash him.'

'Earlier on, up the road there, I saw that young man just passing by when they stopped him and started picking a quarrel. Oh, my! That poor chap's been too badly hurt. It's lucky he's still alive.'

'Why didn't you do something then?'

'How could I know what it was all about? I was just on my way to the chemist's. I was scared, so I went round the other way. When I was coming back I saw them still beating him and urging him to go to the police.' Each of the spectators began loudly to put in a word. The street had been quiet, but now, however they may have found out, people poured in from all the houses buzzing and pushing their way to have a look at Mongdal covered in blood. With the damage to his hair and his clothes that had been scraping along the street and his blood-smeared face, he really did look like a 'mongdal ghost'.

'What is the world coming to? How can people be so evil?'

While Mr Cho was thus lamenting, Mr Kim jumped in again, 'I entirely agree with you. Somehow or other we should have caught those hooligans and handed them over to the police . . .' Then he turned to Mongdal, 'How are you feeling now? What a mess you are in! Let's go, I'll see you home.' He helped him to his feet. Alas, how gutless he was! Instead of shaking off that hand, he just went home supported by Mr Kim.

A few days ago I saw him. It was ten days after. It would be too much bother to tell you how I spent those ten days. When I used to have him around I didn't realize it but now, without him, I was dying of loneliness. I felt as if the day had expanded to forty hours. Now and again, to be honest, I did sit in a chair at the Lucky Super but as I felt estranged from Mr Kim I did not go there often. Not knowing that I had been peeping inside his shop that night, he was as flippant as before.

'Jai-suk, my little sister, why don't we see more of you these days? Don't forget, will you, to let me know as soon as Sun-suk gets home. Then I will give you this. How's that?' What he was waving before me was, as usual, a bar of sweet bean mash. On the wrapper it said 'Nourishing bean jelly' and it was two hundred *won*. He knew I was dying to have one. But, no chance! When Sun-suk comes, I would tell her everything and every detail of his mean and cowardly behaviour so that if there was some slight thread of affection for him left, she would cleanly sever it. For some reason she had not shown so much as the tip of her nose for nearly a month. According to mum, who had gone recently to Seoul, she gets two days off a month from the foreign-goods shop where she works but she doesn't bother to come home. Instead, on these days she stays out all day and crawls back only at night. Apparently my auntie gets phone calls for her from three or four men, or more, and she told my mother that the shop telephone rings for her all the time, enough to melt the line, and the slut is so busy answering them all that she doesn't get any work done. It's clear that my auntie with her peerlessly coarse way of talking, just like that of my mother, has poured out her fault in buckets so that my mother's conclusions, as she came home full of her shortcomings, were just what you'd expect of the 'know-all' of Wonmi.

'That lass, Sun-suk, she's a ruined woman. We might as well make her a movie star or something like that. To be honest, she's better looking than Chang Mi-hi, the latest favourite – don't you think so?'

'You must be mad, quite mad. Do you think anyone can become a star just like that? What a lot of rubbish you talk.' Even though he attacked my mother like this, my father usually ended up by laughing. It was the kind of laugh that meant that in a family with too many daughters it is not too bad a thing if one of them can earn a living by selling her looks.

'The people in Seoul – they have a good eye for looks. Apparently they follow her in crowds, as soon as she appears in Myong-dong, urging her to become a film actress. She's very annoyed about it saying she couldn't care less about her looks . . .' Sometimes my mother, without a blush, would pour out such tales to Kohung Auntie, and Kohung Auntie, still believing Dong-a's eyes to be set on higher things, would start to brag about her so as not to be outdone. 'Our Dong-a – she's learning to play the piano these days and goes to classes on flower-arrangement as well. She's so busy. In this day and age, they say such accomplishments are very important.'

My mother was bad enough, but Kohung Auntie's words made me very uncomfortable. If Dong-a marries that rough young man from the Daishin Facilities, she won't have any chance to arrange flowers, not even a single marrow flower, let alone play the piano. If you look closely at grown-ups you will agree with me that they are often like idiots who know only one thing. The way they talked about Mr Kim after that event is one such example.

'Mr Kim, he really is a good sort. It's only yesterday, I think, he went to see young Mongdal and took him a tin of peaches. He constantly worries about him. To care like that for a man who, whatever you say, is mad, is a proof of his extraordinary good nature.' Mr Cho of the Paper Shop was talking like this to Mr Um of the Photo Studio. Um always treats Cho as an elder brother because he is three years his senior, and when I saw him nodding in agreement with Cho and encouraging him on, I felt my heart would burst. Nevertheless, for some reason, I couldn't speak openly about what happened that night. It must be because I – Jai-suk Kim – am the best of all the good sort of people.

I meant to talk about Mr Mongdal's getting out of bed but yet again I have wandered off. Anyway he really was strange. It must have been shortly after midday, for Nora had just gone home in a hurry, saying she had to get ready for school, which was in the afternoon. On my way home I looked in the direction of the Lucky Super and saw Mongdal, dripping with sweat, engaged in neatly piling up crates of drinks. After being thoroughly beaten up and staying in bed for ten days his face was so pale and emaciated that I could hardly bear to look at it. Even so he kept breaking into smiles as if he was pleased with something as he eagerly carried the crates. And at Mr Kim's shop of all places. I opened my eyes wider to make sure. It was no mistake, it was him. How could he? He was obviously out of his mind, I thought. Even though I knew he was a little mad, he could not possibly work like that unless he had completely forgotten Mr Kim's behaviour on that night.

Could he have forgotten? Could it be that because of his head injury part of his memories of Kim's deeds had been completely wiped out? It was not altogether a wild guess. I remembered watching a TV serial in which, owing to something called amnesia, a father did not recognize even his own son. Talking of imagination of this kind, there is no other child whose imagination could match up with mine for my head is always full of all sorts of strange, weird ideas, packed as tight as a sandbag. I have long since grown out of such childish ideas as that I was not really the daughter of a rubbish man but the abandoned daughter of some great family. These days my imagination turns rather to something of a more mature taste such as seeing myself as the result of love between an extraterrestrial father and an earthly mother. Anyway, by my brilliant imagining Mongdal was diagnosed as a patient suffering from a partial loss of memory. The only thing that was left was to test whether my judgement was right. There was no need to wait any longer. I went across to where he sat under the beach parasol after helping Mr Kim around the shop. He was reading something and I could tell without looking that it was one of the pieces of paper he carried about in his pocket. How pathetic, I thought. On top of his already confused mind, he has added a disease called loss of memory, and he is still reading nothing but poems.

'Another poem?' I said.

'Yes. A sad one, very sad . . .' He broke into a happy smile as he lifted his wan face. Fancy – to smile after talking about a sad poem. I frowned as I went and sat next to him, and in a very low voice I asked. 'Are you all right now?'

'Um. I was laid up reading poems, so I got better quickly.' What did he mean by 'quickly'? It had taken all of ten days. Once again I despaired of his hopeless mental state.

'I was sitting here that night and I saw everything.'

'What did you see?'

'Mr Kim turning you out, uncle . . .' Momentarily his face sobered as he looked into mine. His eyes were not dim, as they had been of late, they shone dark and bright. But it was only for a brief moment. As if determined not to meet my eyes he pretended he was busy removing some scabs on his arm. I drew closer.

'Kim is a bad man. Isn't that so?'

He slapped me on the wrist as he said, 'No.' But I went on harassing him. 'You know that, don't you? I am right, aren't I?'

Even then he pretended not to hear and kept on rubbing his elbow. Like an idiot. It wasn't loss of memory after all . . . I was getting more and more agitated and could bear it no longer, and he tried a different tune. 'This is a sad poem. Do you want to hear it?'

Phooey. Did he think I wanted to listen to such a thing? Regardless of whether or not I thrust out my lower lip he was reciting it.

. . . A silvery aspen yonder,
Its dry twigs invoking the wind within its own body and mind,
is like a martyr under persecution.
Yet on the second view, the silvery aspen yonder,
Like a martyr desiring persecution . . .

'You can read, can't you?' he said. 'You may as well keep this as I now know it all by heart.' He thrust upon me a crumpled piece of paper, saying it was a very sad poem. It did not look sad to me at all but I kept feeling as if I would burst into tears. Like an idiot, and he had known it all along . . . silly Mr Mongdal . . .

The poems quoted in this story are by Kim Chong-whan, Yi Ha-sok and Hwang Ji-woo, in order of appearance.

# SNOWY ROAD

## Yi Chong-jun

### I

'I think we had better go early tomorrow.'

I spat out at last the words that had gone on turning round in my mouth, as I sat back from the lunch table. The old woman and my wife both looked across at me blankly, their spoons suspended in mid air.

'What do you mean early tomorrow? You mean you're going to leave again so soon?' The old lady eventually put down her spoon and repeated the question incredulously. But the die was cast. Now that I had gone this far, I thought, I had better make my position quite clear.

'Yes, I must go tomorrow morning. I am not like a lucky student on holiday, I can't be so idle while the others are working. Besides, there are a couple of things that have to be dealt with at once.'

'Even so, you ought to stay for a few days . . . as you have chosen a time like this, I thought you would be staying on to have a good rest . . .'

'You should know that I am not in any position to come and go as I choose.'

'Even so, it's such a pity that you have to go back so soon after coming such a long way. You always turn up only to go away the next morning . . . this time you are not alone . . . why can't you stay one more night and have a good rest?'

'I have had a restful day today, haven't I? One day's rest takes up three days, you see, because even though the roads are much better now, it is a thousand *li* to Seoul, and it takes a day to get here and another to go back . . .'

'You could have sorted out the urgent business before we came . . .' Instead of the old lady, it was now my wife who gave me a reproachful glance. She could not be blaming me for bad planning. Before we left, I had told her that I had got all the pressing matters out of the way. I was the one who had suggested that this time we would take a few days out of our summer leave, to look up the old lady with more time to spare. She was rather blaming me for my impatience and my change of heart. She made it clear through the expression of pity and pleading in her eyes that she resented my heartlessness.

After sitting quietly for a while the old lady said resignedly, 'Of course, if you are really pressed for time you'll have to go. What's the point in detaining a man who has urgent things to do? I know you are always busy. It's just that as your mother I felt bad about not being able to provide you with a comfortable bed when you came to see me before – that's all.'

When she had finished, she began to fill the little bowl at the end of her long pipe, pressing the tobacco down firmly with a nonchalant expression. It was too easy a resignation. Unlike my wife, there was no trace of resentment in her face as she kept on cramming the tobacco into the bowl. Nor was there any sign of wistfulness over her heartless son who was fidgeting to get away from her. She didn't strike a match but went on packing in the tobacco, the expression in her eyes remote and unconcerned. I felt irritated by her indifference and easy acceptance. At last I got to my feet, and as if being pushed out by her attitude, walked out of the room. In the garden, outside the sliding door stood a cape jasmine enduring the fierce midday sun.

## 2

It was throbbing with heat in the bean field behind the house, and in the middle of it was a grave surrounded by thriving alders. Sitting well hidden in the shade, I looked back at the house down the slope of the field. It looked more like a mushroom that had sprung up in a damp spot in summer. I felt nervous as if an obligation might suddenly crop up from somewhere.

It had been the fault of the tiny and damp, single-roomed hut to begin with. It aroused in me an uneasiness that some old debt might thrust itself out, and so it made me change our plan and decide to go straight back. Even so, I was certain that there was no debt to be paid. As far as the old woman was concerned there was no question of my owing her anything. My position was as clear as could be, and, she herself was perfectly aware of it.

'I am nearly seventy now. Even if I live on, how much longer will I last?' That was what she had said. It had been some time ago. As her teeth had completely rotted away, eating became very troublesome. Realizing that, I had suggested, as if in passing, that she might like some dentures, if only cheap ones. Probably she didn't see much hope in my verbal charity and declined on the spot. 'Somehow or other I shall carry on as I am. I have no wish for my life to be any different.'

At another time she had had bad haemorrhoids, and emptying her bowels was extremely painful. I had urged her to have an operation. That time also she gave a similar reply. 'However old, I am still a woman. How can I put my unsightly parts before someone else's eyes? Somehow or other I shall put up with it until I finally go . . .' It was partly due to her belief that she had not long to live, but more because she was aware that she was in no position to have any claim on me, nor expect any reward.

It had been like this ever since my first year at High School, when my family had been made bankrupt through my elder brother's drinking habits. After that he died and I was left with all the responsibilities and duties of an eldest son, including the care of his three children and their widowed mother. Through my High-School years, the time at college, and then the further three years of the military service, the old lady could not fulfil even the least part of the duties of a parent. On my side, even after leaving school and the army, I had not performed any of the duties of a decent son, not because she had done little for me but simply because I could not. I was quite unable to carry out the duties that had been pushed upon me by my brother. In this way we found ourselves in a situation in which we had no claims on each other whatsoever. The old lady knew this better than anyone. She could not expect anything from me nor bear resentment. She had accepted this, but this time, for some reason, I sensed something odd about her. Could it be that she who had resolutely declined such offers as dentures or an operation, had now found some new hope of life at an age only two years short of eighty? She seemed to be dreaming some wild dream – a very wild one.

It had been the roof-improvement campaign that was to blame in the first place. 'They are putting slates or tiles on their roofs, that's what it is.' She had started off as if she was just talking about other people's affairs. It was shortly before the three of us got into bed on the night before. When it was quite late, my sister-in-law had gone over to a neighbour's to sleep, taking her three children with her, and the three of us had laid out our bedding in that one small room. At that moment the noise of men working somewhere came, 'upsa, upsa', and it grew louder and louder. After listening awhile I asked her what it was. She started to talk about it quite casually.

'Everybody in the village has gone mad trying to improve their houses, even giving up their sleep for it.' There was a 'Campaign for Renewing Roofs' going on, she told us. Since the introduction of the new type of rice, 'Tong-il rice', which yielded better crops, thatching became difficult because the stalks were shorter than the traditional straw. Indeed, the improvement that had started in the early spring looked quite good. She went on to tell us that if you wanted to change your roof you could get a government subsidy of fifty thousand *won*. The work could only be carried out during the short spell in spring before the rice planting began or in the early summer after it was over. Nevertheless, the result was that nearly all the houses in the village had been done.

When she started talking about it, my heart missed a beat without rhyme or reason. It was at that moment that the thought of some debt to her came to my head – what was I going to do if this old woman got some absurd idea into her head? But I was able to calm myself down. Nothing could be clearer than the fact that I did not owe her anything. She could in no way have forgotten that. I was absolutely sure that she would never betray such an unreasonable wish to a son such as I was. I had trusted her in this way before. It was part of her personality. Besides, even if she should harbour some unreasonable hope, the state of the house would render it out of the question. Apart from the question of slates or tiles, the house itself was not up to repairs to the roof. I gathered that in one way or another she had not dared to hold out any hope. But I had been mistaken. It now dawned on me that her inner thoughts could have been otherwise.

'If it was an official drive, they must have come to see you about it several times, mustn't they?' It was a slip of the tongue on my part to put in these idle words as a gesture of consolation. I had been over-optimistic about the situation. The old lady sat up in bed for the second time, and started cramming a handful of tobacco into the bowl at the end of her long pipe.

'There's no reason why our house should escape the trouble, is there?' Again she spoke in a neutral tone of voice, as if it was someone else's affair. 'The head of the village rushed in and took his time trying to persuade me, then a district officer came with a threat . . . it was not just once or twice . . . in the end they begged for my cooperation.'

'So how did you stick it out?' I still did not know her true intention.

'There's nothing to stick out for, is there? Those fellows were human beings with human eyes. They could see for themselves . . . when they were appealing for my sympathy I asked for theirs too. I said, "Though old, I am just like anyone else. Do you think I don't want to live in a good house? A thousand, ten thousand times, I have wished I could put some tiles on the roof and replace those pillars, but just have a look at the state of the house itself. An earthen hut like this, how could you expect me to put tiles on it?" '

'Then what happened?'

'They called a few more times, and then they gradually left off talking about it. After all they are not blind, are they? When they saw the house, even they couldn't fail to grasp the situation.' She kept pressing on the hot end of her pipe with her rough thick thumb.

'It looks as though they had their mind set on making this a model village by achieving one hundred per cent roof renovation.' Feeling somewhat bitter and sad, I was going to pass over the subject in this ambiguous way. But that was a fatal slip.

'That's right. They were saying something about how after the house they are working on tonight, ours and Sunsim's, down the road, will be the only two that are not renovated. That's what they said.'

'Even so, they can't really force you to put tiles on a house like this, can they? Just for the sake of getting the title of a "model village." '

'I don't know. I feel that if it was just a matter of putting on slates or tiles, I would dare to give it a try, but the thing is that a house like this needs the whole of the wooden framework redoing . . .' With the term 'model village' becoming yet another starting-point, I realized that the conversation was expanding into a further unknown area. My heart was by now positively smarting, but it was too late to retreat.

'In many cases, roof renovation is only a name. Lots of people take the opportunity to go on and do up the whole framework.' Once she had got going she went on with more details of the situation in the village.

The so-called roof renovation project had, I realized, a wide range of possibilities and implications. The principle was to remove the thatched roof and replace it with tiles or slates, but to withstand the weight of the tiles many houses had to have several beams replaced, and taking this occasion as an excuse, most people went on to replace the frame and improve the foundations, and altogether they ended up by rebuilding their houses. My old lady had received much encouragement to do something like this. The only excuse she had for turning it down was that the beams of her house were too worn to take the weight of the tiles. Three other houses had put off the tile replacement on the grounds of the beams being too feeble, but one of them where the work went on into today, was now having its frame reinforced. The reason she had turned the offer down was not the weakness of the rafters but the enormous cost of replacing the ridge-beam.

I could no longer count on the weakness of the beams, and could not be optimistic about getting out of it. Suddenly I found myself preoccupied with calculating what I owed her. She, meanwhile, seemed to be concentrating on the dwindling fire in her long pipe. Then at last she let out a faint sigh as if she found it hard to repress her hopes any longer. She spoke at the end of it, words that sounded indifferent.

'While at it, I thought, it would be nice to add another room and do up the roof with slates, but . . .' Finally she was revealing what she had hoped at that time. 'You never know whether you might not die today or tomorrow, but as I go on hanging on to my tenacious life, not worth as much as a bird's, all sorts of thoughts come up. I haven't even got enough space to keep that chest of drawers, so I have to push it about from here to there. Sometimes it tempted me like a honey cake to get it done . . .'

In this way the old lady made her wishes very clear. It might not be her present expectation but it was obvious that she had once cherished such hopes. I had nothing to say now. With my eyes closed I just listened to her. I repeated to myself for the hundredth time that I owed her nothing.

'This time the village office let me off, but I don't know whether they will keep quiet next year. Come to think of it, it is not really for them that we improve our house, is it? Also, I can't overlook the problem of the mother and the children.' She was referring to my three nephews and their widowed mother. 'She probably can't stand the smell of an old woman like me. You'd think there was enough room for all of us to lie down on our backs, but she goes out every night to sleep next door.'

No longer getting any response from me, she went on as if talking to herself. Listening to her I realized that she had a fairly well constructed plan in her mind.

'The subsidy from the government is as much as 50,000 *won*. Once the work is started and under way, what could there be that needed big money? . . . Without men in the family, I knew, it wouldn't be easy to get hold of labour. But if your sister-in-law had agreed to look after the crop in the field just for the summer, people like Yongsok's dad, for example, wouldn't turn their backs and ignore us . . .' She went on to say that she could have asked Yongsok's dad to look after the clay work, and that the village headman would have let her have some wood for the beams cheaply from his plantation. The fire had gone out at the end of her pipe and it was cool. As she kept on sucking at the cold pipe, she was saying how hard it had been to give it up, what with the 50,000 *won* subsidy and the likely help of the neighbours. However, she still did not show any sign of making a claim on me, nor any sign of resentfulness. The way she spoke of it, it was an affair of the past, just what she had felt about it at that time and how she had nearly done it. And in this way she was obviously trying to spare me from feeling a burden in any way. Her tone of voice throughout was characteristic of her unperturbed calmness, deeply tinged with resignation.

'But it is all useless. If things in this world went as you wished who would be afraid of getting old? As they say when you are old, you are like a child. It was just an old woman's madness . . .' In the end she denounced even her most cherished hopes as due to her aged dementia. But this time I could not fail to perceive what lay in her heart. Even my wife, lying quietly without putting in one word and feigning sleep, had clearly understood it.

'Was that all you could say to your mother last night?' She quietly rebuked me this morning when she saw me as she came out to the yard with a basin of water to wash her face. I gave her a sharp glance as if to say, 'Mind your own business.' At this she accused me rather contemptuously, 'You are harder than you need to be. Don't you feel sorry for her? I think you should have comforted her generously, at least in words.' She had obviously taken in what my mother had said, and was more concerned about her than I was. Clearly she had also been probing every nook and cranny in my feelings towards my mother. That was why she had cautiously showed her disapproval of my sudden decision to go back to Seoul. But what wonderful idea was there for her to come up with?

One thing that was clear was that even now my mother would still like to rebuild the house. I could not, for the life of me, understand it. It must be true that as one grows old one becomes a child again. Had she really forgotten that I owed her nothing? As she herself admitted, it must be dementia. There was no need for me to blame her for mental disorientation. It was only a question of my debt. That I was not in debt to her was all that mattered. If she became shameless or mentally disordered, it did not matter as long as there was no debt to be paid off – and of course there's absolutely nothing! You could see that the old lady knew that. That's why she could not bring it up directly to my face.

From somewhere came the sultry, idle cries of the cicada. As if I had consolidated my belief quite firmly, I determinedly raised myself from the shadow of the silver birch. Down beyond the slopes of the bean plantation the village stretched out, and I could see the old lady's hut. The lone thatched roof like a poisonous fungus, and further down another in the neighbourhood.

'Damn it all! The blessed "Roof Renovation Scheme" or whatever you call it! Why did it have to come up just at this time and cause such a fuss?'

Whatever I thought to myself, I could not feel cheerful. Vainly I put the blame on the innocent project of roof renovation.

It was only after the sun had sunk much lower that I went back across the bean plot into the backyard of the house. When I looked into it I found my wife was engaged in an unsavoury conversation with my mother.

'It would be silly to think of adding a new room and putting tiles on the roof with the hope of a better life for myself at this age . . . it's not greed for the house itself, but just that I can't help thinking about after I have gone . . .'

As I walked round towards the front, I caught the drone of my mother's voice from the half-open door of her room.

'If it was spring, with fresh weather, or even summer, when an awning could be put up in the courtyard, I wouldn't worry so much. But just think, if my breath goes out with a gasp in the middle of the winter. With my body laid out in full at one end of a single room, what can you do?'

It was a conversation about the house again. How did she think she could offer any comfort to my mother? Or was it that no longer able to turn away from the hopes of the old lady, she meant to bring them up to the surface? Was her feeling towards my cautious approach as deep and prudent as that? It was obvious that my wife had led my mother up to that point. The old lady was now expressing her wishes in a clear-cut voice, and giving clear reasons for them. With the strength of her habitual resignation and sense of honour her wishes had been hesitantly subsiding again, but now they were being fully revealed. I had had some idea of them but I had never expected to encounter such a clear explanation. I felt as if my last hope had collapsed, yet I was glad of it, as it made a certain point very clear to me. It was the source of that extraordinary ambition of hers that she seemed suddenly to have acquired. Her hopes were not for her own comfort but about the things to come after her death.

'Even though I had originally drifted into this village, I had never done any harm to anyone until I reached this age. I have eaten poorly, dressed roughly and slept in a rough bed in my old age, but I have never been treated badly by the neighbours or the villagers. What I mean by this is that when I die, the people will come at least to throw a handful of soil, or add a piece of turf over my dead body. What should I do for them, the young and the old who would come to see me in this way? Nothing can be worse than being troubled in your death. I can't say "No" to those who come to see me, and I should like to offer them at least a cup of wine. Is it asking too much? That's what I have been thinking about to myself. Unless I am taken out and buried the day I breathe my last, there is only one room for the dead and the living between them, and that includes you two who would have come a long way . . . So I had been hoping to fix up one more room just to keep the wind out and to sit down . . . but it's not as easy as one thinks, is it? This or that, it's all the madness of a silly old woman . . .'

Her wishes had arisen in readiness for her death. I could understand that. Since our home had been ruined and consequently she had to leave our old village to drift about in the world, she had always been mindful of the arrangements in the face of her death. She had even obtained from an old man a 'site for my house' as she called her grave space in a sunny spot at the foot of the hill behind the village, and even in winter, when the weather was fine, she would go there to enjoy the warm sun – I had known this of her. Now she was hastening the last preparations for her death. I could no longer bear to hear her talking and I was about to move quietly away when suddenly it seemed that my wife, who is prone to be easily moved even by trifling things, could endure it no longer. She abruptly changed the subject and said, 'Mother, I've heard that the house where you used to live was a big one with many rooms, is that right?' Not being able to find words to comfort her, she must have chosen to soothe her by recalling her memories of the large house, probably attempting to change her mood by reminding her that once she had run a well-to-do household. It might also help to restore her pride in relation to a daughter-in-law who on her visits had seen only her poor and shameful condition. Anyway, my urge to get away from the scene had now gone.

'Oh, the old house. It was enormous. Two sets of five rooms each with courtyards in front and behind as big as a school field . . . But what good does that do now? It's nearly twenty years since it became somebody else's . . .'

'But you once lived in such a grand house, so you must have some pleasant memories, don't you, mother? When you are fed up with this little house, try to bring back those memories.'

'What's the use of memories? There are times anyway, when

they come back vividly one after another. It makes me feel quite restless.'

'Yes, I can understand that. When you think about those days in the big house, the present circumstances would make you feel bad, as it's such a contrast to this little place . . .'

The old lady and my wife went on talking like this for some time. It was hard to say whether it was reassurance or grumbling. As I was listening to it, I began to feel more and more suspicious of my wife's motives. From the way she spoke, it did not sound as if she wanted to comfort my mother, but rather to provoke her by making her feel uncomfortable. Reminding her of her old home, rather than calming her fretfulness, was making her feel more intensely discontented with her present life. It was bringing to the surface her concealed desire to renovate the house – it seemed as though that was my wife's intention. My guess proved to be not far from the truth.

'The room is so small as it is, mother. Couldn't you put this chest somewhere else? It takes up too much space in a room that's already too small.' She was drawing the conversation on to the point where I felt most uncomfortable and even tried to avert my eyes. There was a history attached to that big chest of drawers. It went back seventeen or eighteen years to when I was a first-year student away at High School in the town. The news reached me that my elder brother, whose drinking problem was worsening, and who had already sold our land and the hill which was our ancestral burial ground, had finally sold the house itself. I was to spend my winter vacation in the town but I wanted to find out how things were at home, so I went back. I had not expected to see the family there now that the house had been sold but there were other sources from which I could get news. I waited until dusk before I entered the alley where it was. It was as I had heard. It was empty and the family nowhere to be seen. I went to the home of a distant cousin who also lived in the same lane. She told me, to my surprise, that my mother was still waiting there for me.

'Where do you think you are? How come you dither around in the alley in front of your own gate like this, my son?' This was how she scolded me when, having heard from my cousin that I was there, she came running out from somewhere and saw me hesitantly peering into the yard. Half-believing, I went over the threshold, though the house had obviously been sold. That night she cooked my supper exactly as in the past and spent the night there with me. The next day, at dawn, she saw me off to the town. I found out much later that she had so much wanted to give me one last meal and let me pass the night at the old house that she had asked permission from the new owner and had been waiting for me. She had not known when I would come, but she wanted to see me spending one last night surrounded by familiar sights and atmosphere of the old days. But as soon as I stepped in I could sense the air of a house from which the family had moved out. Nevertheless, until that day, she had come in and out to dust and clean it. And as a token of preserving the old life, she had kept, as in the old days, a set of bedding and a chest of clothes at one side of the family room.

When I was setting off for the town early next morning she clearly explained the fact that the house had been sold, and I fully appreciated her wish to console me on this sorrowful night by reviving the old atmosphere with the chest. This is the history behind that box. In her wandering life obviously she had not been able to collect any other furniture. This was all she had been able to preserve through the past twenty years or so. On the other hand, it had always been an object that made me feel uncomfortable. I would swear to myself that I owed her nothing, but when I saw it I would feel very upset as if I was faced with a bill for some unspecified amount. It had happened again this time. From the moment I first entered the room it had made me feel uncomfortable. Come to think of it, it was largely because of that box that, feeling unable to stay for another night, I had decided to go back.

Of course my wife had heard all about the box from me. Knowing its history, it was unimaginable that she would not know of my feelings about it. As she went on talking, it might well be that she knew I was listening. I became so tense that, unaware of it, my bad habit of picking my nose came back. I was fretting as if quite unexpectedly an old unpaid bill might pop up from somewhere. It was possible that the old woman was shameless and trying to drive me into a corner.

'I don't care. However you try to catch me I am absolutely clear of debt, and you can't just make one up out of nothing.'

As if in prayer, I lightly closed my eyes and waited. Then came a fortunate reply from the old woman, who throughout had looked unconcerned. 'If I move it out, where am I supposed to keep my few items of clothing? Not that there is anywhere else to put it, but even if there were, I still need somewhere to keep my few clothes, don't I?' Whether consciously or not, my mother did not seem to be over-concerned about the chest itself.

'You can always hammer in a few nails to hang your clothes on, can't you? More than anything else, you need enough space for people to lie down with their legs stretched out. You sound as though you take the chest more seriously than the people.' My wife was almost absurdly persistent. It seemed clear that she was setting out to test the old woman's attachment to the chest. But my mother's reaction was the same as before.

'You say that because you don't understand. If there wasn't even a chest in sight, who would call this a house for people? As a token of human living it must be kept indoors.'

'You must be very attached to it, mother. Is there some history behind it? Is it one that you brought with you when you were married?' Because of my mother's advanced age, my wife often acted playfully like a saucy little granddaughter. Now she was full of it.

'History? Not in particular . . .' With that she closed her mouth. Probably she did not want to talk about the chest any more. But my wife is not one to be easily put off by such a retreat. When the old lady did not answer, she also fell silent as if lost for words, but in the end she launched a new onslaught. 'Well, I can see that your heart can't be at peace. After all, your happiest days must have been when you were running the old house. How did it come about that it had to be sold?'

They were back to the house again. And it was not as if my wife did not know about it. Indeed, she knew all the history attached to the chest and the circumstances in which the house had to be sold. And yet she was making the old lady tell it all again. It was a furthering of her endeavour – talking about the chest was a means of bringing to the surface the old lady's wishes. And the old woman's attitude was as tenacious as my wife's.

'What do you mean "How did it come about . . .". Do you think I sold the house for the fun of it? It was just that I was not fated to have a house . . .' The question had been put by my wife with full knowledge, and my mother was trying to wriggle out of answering it.

'Even so, there must have been some reason, mustn't there? I've heard that my late father-in-law took a lot of trouble with the building of it.'

'That's true. It was a house earned by hard work. It was not like some people who build a whole house at one go – it took us several years as we went on adding a room now and again, depending on our circumstances, you see. The house we built in that way, in the end, didn't remain ours . . . but what's the use of talking about it? It was just fated not to be mine, that's all there is to it. Harping on it is not going to bring back the house.'

'More's the pity when it was a hard-won house, isn't it? And your present situation makes it seem such a shame. Wouldn't you really like to talk about how it all happened and what things were like at the time?'

'No, dear. It's all useless. Besides, such a long time has passed since then – even my memories are faint . . .'

'Very well, mother. I reckon you are being like this because you think there is no point in upsetting me with what went on in the past. You don't need to be, for, to tell the truth, I have already heard about it, though only roughly, so I do understand.' As my mother still persisted in avoiding telling the truth, my wife had launched this as a final assault.

'Heard about it? From whom?' At last she betrayed some surprise.

'From him of course, who else?'

I had kept out of sight, but her tone of voice made it clear that she was referring to me, the one listening to their conversation. It was also obvious that she had been aware of my overhearing them from outside.

'Not only do I know the circumstances in which it was sold, but I also know about what you did to enable him to spend one last night in the house after it was sold. I feigned ignorance, but I know about that chest of clothes too. You kept that old piece of furniture in the house to make him believe that you were still there. That's what he told me.' For no apparent reason her voice had a tremor. 'If that was the case, mother, why don't you open your heart to us and speak freely. Instead of trying to bear up and endure it all alone, speak freely to your heart's content. We are your children, aren't we? Why do you want to conceal your heart even from your own offspring.'

Her voice was almost choking with tears. There was a long silence instead of a reply from the old lady, as if she had reached her wits' end. As for me, the inside of my mouth was parched. How would my mother respond? I held my breath and waited for her next words. Regardless of the anxiety of myself and my wife, her reply was quite unperturbed.

'I see. So the boy still remembers that night?'

'Of course he does. And that night as he restlessly loitered up and down the lane unable to bring himself to enter the house, you took him inside, didn't you, as if the house hadn't been sold, and made him supper, is that right?'

'That's right then. You knew all about it, so what do you want me to repeat it for?'

'You see, he has almost forgotten, and I can't get the true story out of him. He is so hard and tries to forget things like that. So this time I want to hear from you, mother, the real truth, not his account but your own account of how you felt that night.'

'As for my feelings or whatever you call it, there isn't much to add to what he told you. Even though the house had been sold in unavoidable circumstances, my feet hadn't stopped coming and going there, and when I saw my child walking up and down past the house with uncertain steps . . .'

No longer able to defy my wife's solicitations, she was recounting what had happened in a rather reluctant tone of voice. It still did not betray her real feelings. 'So I scolded him as I hurried him into the house. Then I cooked a meal for him and put him up for the night in his old house, and the following day, even before the dawn, sent him away . . .'.

'How did you feel as you did so?'

'What do you think? Even though the house had been sold I had so much wished that I could have him there for one last night. As I waited for him I went up and down that hateful alley to sweep the garden and clean the floors of the house. So when I had given him the last hot meal and the last night's sleep, I felt as if at last my one wish had been granted.'

'Are you saying then, that you were satisfied as you sent him away? It couldn't be that, could it? You couldn't be happy when you saw him off, could you? At least he had his school to go back to, but for you, you could not even afford to find some meagre lodgings for yourself.'

'What more do you want me to tell you, child?'

'Please tell me about your state of mind when you were sending him away – your mental state when you had to send away your son in such a manner with you yourself having no roof over your head and faced with a life of aimless wandering. What was it like?'

'You don't want it, dear. It would be pointless. Even if I told you you couldn't understand it. How could you?' Once again she declined to talk. But now in her tone some resignation was seeping in. One might have detected some remains of a story that she alone had kept in her heart. I could wait no longer. My wife was conscious of my presence, though the old lady was not. I had to stop her saying any more. However much she was pressured by my wife, there are things that she would not like me to know. She was not to continue with her talk. At last I gave a false cough as I thrust myself into the spot in front of the sliding door where her eyes were resting.

## 4

One way or another the crisis points had been got over. When the supper table was brought in she ordered a measure of *makkuli*, rice wine, to accompany it. When you think about it, it was my brother's drinking that brought the family to such a state, but, amazingly, my mother did not worry about me drinking. Whenever I went home, she had a measure or two of *makkuli* that she had herself bought in readiness for me.

'Drink a cup and have a good sleep,' she would say. She'd always encouraged me to sleep. It was the same this evening. When the supper was brought in she asked me in a cautious voice. 'So, do you really mean to go early tomorrow morning?'

'When I say I must go, obviously there must be some work that calls me.' I spoke gracelessly in a somewhat angry tone of voice. She said, 'That's all right. Have your supper with some wine, and then go to bed early.' If you are to set off early on a long journey you'd better to be in bed early – that was what she meant. I followed her instructions. After eating my supper, and emptying the little bottle of wine, I spread out my bedding and lay down, pretending to be overcome by the alcohol. My sister-in-law went out with her three children to their sleeping place in the neighbourhood, and again the three of us were to spend the night together. Anyway, we were more or less past the peak of the crisis. I closed my eyes. When I opened them again, it would all be over. The roof and the chest and whatever else there was, they would no longer pester my nerves. Suppose the old lady had some record of debt tucked away? Even so, get through this night safely and it would be no more than waste paper.

'Go to sleep. Once you are asleep debt or whatever else there might be can't hurt you. My debt to the old lady? That's nonsense . . .'. I was almost in a light mood as I closed my eyes and called for sleep. Perhaps because of the influence of the alcohol, a numbing slumber came pressing on my eyelids.

How long had I been wandering in the comforting world of sleep? For some reason I was aware that it was slowly lifting, and in the semi-consciousness of a light sleep I could hear the drone of the old woman talking in a cautious tone of voice. '. . . It so happened that during the night, unexpectedly, thick snow fell. I could not have slept very long but just closed my eyes for a while. When I got up near dawn and looked out, it was a world of snow . . . it must not stop us from going out. Hastily I cooked some rice to warm our insides, and then in a hurry we set out on the snowy road . . .'. Somehow it had come about that she was in the middle of telling my wife the story of that night, item by item.

'If our situation had been better we could at least have waited until the daybreak, but I felt so ashamed and resentful about it. So we set out on the snowy road at dawn. How long it seemed, those three miles of hilly road to the bus station in the town.' As she calmly retraced her memories, her dreamy voice had the cosiness of a grandmother telling her grandchild a fairy tale. It seemed as if my wife had finally led her on to that point.

'Even if I told you, you wouldn't understand. How could you possibly?' In their daytime conversation, my mother had left some loose ends by declining to say any more and my wife could not let it rest. In the night, or rather at dawn, my mother was ruminating on the events of the snowy road on that other dawn that I had never spoken of to my wife, and that I had hoped would disappear for ever beyond the shores of my memory. She spoke in an ineffectual voice as if rummaging through the documents of some debt that was for ever beyond the means of retrieving.

'It was dark all around and the steep paths were rough. Slipping and falling over, somehow we managed to get to the bus station on time . . .'. In my mind's eye, as I listened to her, the scenes of that day floated so vividly as to seem within touching distance. Probably she had felt much pity for her young son leaving in that way, or sorry for herself in her poor circumstances. When we set off, she said she would go with me as far as the end of the village, but when we got there she insisted on going on to the brow of the hill. When we were there, she insisted that we went over the hill together until we came to the new main road. Each time it happened we had a brief argument, and after that we could find no words. True, it would have been better if it had been lighter, but it had never occurred to either of us to wait for daybreak before we set out. All we had thought was that it would be best to leave the village in the dark. As she was now telling my wife, we slipped and fell. When she slipped, I steadied her, and when I fell over, she picked me up again, and in this way, without words, we reached the main road. From there the bus station was still quite a long way. She ended up by walking with me all the way to the station. It was still before daybreak.

Then what happened? I went on board the bus, and it left, while she turned round to go back along the snowy road in the dark. That was all I knew. I had never heard the details of her return. From the moment I got on the bus, leaving her alone by the roadside, I could not bring myself to think about her any more, and on her side, she had never mentioned to me what happened later that day. Now, today, without rhyme or reason, she was reviving those particular memories.

'Somehow, we managed to get to the market square and from there we could see the station not far off. Just then we saw the bus coming out with its headlights on. In haste, I raised my arm and waved to it to stop. But how impatient and heartless the crew were. It barely stopped, and with a rattling and clanking he was snatched aboard and disappeared in the twinkling of an eye.'

'So what did you do next, mother?' put in my wife, who had been listening in silence all this time. Suddenly I took fright at the old lady's story. I felt an impulse to spring up and interrupt her, but I could not. My limbs would not obey me. My whole body was weighed down like cotton wool soaked in water. I could not make it move. An indescribable sweetish sorrow, a pleasant exhaustion, was gently coming over me.

'What do you think I did? What could I do but stand there and stare down the road where the bus had gone? I stood there in the darkness for a long time like a lost soul. How could I ever describe the empty feeling in my heart . . .?'. Her voice was as calm and gentle as before, as if she was still telling a fairy tale, as she went on recalling what happened that day.

'After standing there for a long time, I recovered my wits a little in the cold wind. When I came to myself, how the thought of going back brought back the empty feeling again. Until now, there had been the two of us, struggling all the way together, but now all by myself going back along the road . . . it was still dark . . . I could not set out as I was. So I went into the bus station. I squatted on one of the wooden benches in the waiting room for about an hour or so until the sky in the east became lighter . . . then I set off alone. There was no need to hurry now. All my life I will never forget what followed.'

'You mean the time while you were going back?'

'As I retraced the snowy road, I noticed that no one else had been along it since the two of us. The snow had stopped and all the way along the road I saw it was marked with the footprints we two had made, walking side by side.'

'It must have made you think more keenly of your son.'

'More keenly? It's not just that. As I left the main road and turned on to the winding hilly path, those wretched footprints were still there, and I felt as if in them there still lingered the murmuring voice of that child and the warmth of his body. If a wood pigeon flew by, I started as I fancied his spirit had come back in the form of a bird. When I saw the snow-covered trees I kept thinking I would see him leaping out from behind them any minute. All the way back through those curving and winding hillside paths, I was following his footmarks. My child, my child, after sending you away, now this useless old woman is going back along this road on which you and I went out together.'

'Didn't you cry, mother?'

'Cry indeed! I scattered tears in every hollow made by his feet. My son, my son, you must take care of yourself, I beg you. I pray with all my heart that of all your family you at least will be lucky and blessed . . . My tears were blinding me as I prayed to God for his future . . .'. Her story was drawing to a close. My wife, as if lost for words, was silent.

'Somehow, my feeble footsteps – there was no need to hurry now – carried me back and I found myself at the hill before the village. But I could not go down it straight away. I swept away the snow from a seat on the brow of it and I sat there for a long time just waiting . . .'.

'You no longer had anywhere to go back to, did you?' My wife, who had kept quiet for some time, suddenly interrupted her, as if she could stand it no longer. Her voice now had a tremor as she fought back her tears. I too could not bear to listen any more. Even now I would have interrupted her. I was too scared to face up to her answer to my wife's questioning. I could not stand it, yet it was impossible to avoid it.

Even now I could not open my eyes. I could not open them to the lamplight and get up. It was not because my body felt paralysed nor because I wanted to hold on to the lingering sleepiness. It was because I could not reveal what surged hot under my eyelids. I was too ashamed of it. I could sense that my wife knew of my struggle.

'Darling!' All of a sudden, she shook me sharply. 'Please wake up. Get up and let us hear what you have to say.' Her voice was near to a tearful hysteria. Still I could not rouse myself. To hide the hot tears I had to persist in feigning sleep as I pressed tight my eyelids. The only one with a still unperturbed voice was the old lady.

'Leave him alone, dear. Why wake a man up when he's fast asleep? He'll be tired enough when he has to set off early in the morning.' After restraining my wife, my mother went on to bring her story to an end, her voice still calm and even. 'I think you misunderstood me on one point. I mean about my sitting on the brow of the hill instead of going straight down into the village. It was not because I did not have anywhere to go. After all, I was still alive and kicking. It would be possible for me to find some place to lay my head even if it was in somebody else's gatehouse. It was because of the rays of the sun, spreading with such brilliance. It was even shining on the snow-covered roof of our old house, and my eyes were dazzled so that I could not see it. Moreover, the breakfast-smoke was rising all over the village. I felt I could not enter it with my eyes dazzled as they were. I was too ashamed of myself to face the transparent rays of the sun and venture into the village. I had to wait until my eyes had cooled down. That's why I was sitting there . . .'.